ST. JOSEPH OF A[...]
AT GLASTON[...]

ST. JOSEPH OF ARIMATHEA AT GLASTONBURY

or

THE APOSTOLIC CHURCH OF BRITAIN

LIONEL SMITHETT LEWIS
late Vicar of Glastonbury

JAMES CLARKE & CO. LTD.
CAMBRIDGE

First edition 1922
Second edition 1923
Third edition 1924
Fourth edition 1927
Fifth edition 1931
Sixth edition 1937
Seventh edition 1955
Reprinted 1976
Paperback edition 1982

ISBN 0 227 67868 0

Published by:
James Clarke & Co Ltd
7 All Saints' Passage
Cambridge, CB2 3LS
England

Printed in Great Britain by
Redwood Burn Limited, Trowbridge,
and bound by Pegasus Bookbinding, Melksham.

AN OLD GLASTONBURY COLLECT

ALMIGHTY, everlasting God, Who didst entrust Thy most
blessed servant, Joseph, to take down the lifeless body of Thine
Only-Begotten Son from the Cross, and to perform the due
offices of humanity, hasten, we pray Thee, that we, who
devotedly recall His memory, may feel the help of Thine
accustomed pity, through the same, Our Lord. Amen.

THE GLASTONBURY HYMN

AND did those feet in ancient time
　　Walk upon England's mountains green?
And was the Holy Lamb of God
　　On England's pleasant pastures seen?
And did the Countenance Divine
　　Shine forth upon our clouded hills?
And was Jerusalem builded here
　　Among those dark Satanic mills?

Bring me my bow of burning gold!
　　Bring me my arrows of desire!
Bring me my spear! O clouds unfold!
　　Bring me my Chariot of Fire!
I will not cease from mental fight,
　　Nor shall my sword sleep in my hand,
Till I have built Jerusalem
　　In England's green and pleasant land.

　　　　　　　　　WILLIAM BLAKE, 1757–1827

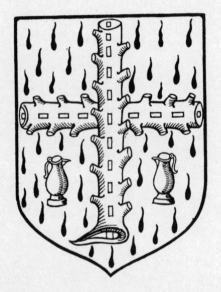

ARMS ACCREDITED TO ST. JOSEPH

CONTENTS

CHAP.   PAGE
1. Antiquity of Glastonbury and Origin of the
    National Church   13

PART II : TRADITIONS

2. St. Joseph of Arimathea   23
3. Good King Lucius   35
4. Our Lord and the Blessed Virgin   51
5. Topical Support of the Traditions   73

PART III : AUTHORITIES

6. The Coming of the Disciples of Christ   85
7. The Coming of St. Joseph of Arimathea   92
8. The Coming of St. Philip to France   112
9. The Coming of St. Simon Zelotes   117
10. The Coming of Aristobulus   118
11. The Coming of St. Paul   122

PART IV : EVIDENCES

12. Early Missions from Britain   127
13. Early Fathers, Diocletian Persecution, Church
    Councils, and Pelagian Heresy   129
14. Conclusion   142

    Appendices   151

CHAPTER I

ANTIQUITY OF GLASTONBURY
AND
ORIGIN OF THE NATIONAL CHURCH

GLASTONBURY has been successively previously called Ynnis-witrin, Isle of Avilion, and Isle of Avalon. John Harding in his Chronicle (temp. Edw. IV) says that it was also constantly called Mewtryen or Mewtryne.[1] But the well-known names are Ynnis-witryn, Avalon, and Glastonbury. Ynnis-witryn is generally supposed to be crystal or glassy isle; Isle of Avilion, isle of departed spirits; Isle of Avalon, isle of apples (the latter being a Saxon corruption of Avilion), and certainly the place excels in apples. It is not strictly correct to pronounce the *t* in Glastonbury, and it has often been spelt Glassenbury. If the usual interpretation of Ynnis Witryn, Glassy or Crystal Isle be accepted, the *en* in Glassenbury may well be *ynnis* or *ennis*, and Glassen a muddled corruption of Ynnis (isle), Witryn (crystal), with the Saxon *bury* or borough tacked on. Such jumbles of different languages do take place in English place names. For instance some three miles from Glastonbury are West Pennard and West Pennard Hill. *Pen* means hill, and *ard* means hill, and so when we say West Pennard Hill we are using three languages to call it

---

[1] It is rather interesting that Melchinus Avalonius, a prophet, poet, historian, and astronomer (Maelgwyn of Avalon) was called Meuin. He flourished about 560. Pitsaeus names three books of his: (1) of British antiquities; (2) of the Acts of the Britons; (3) of the round table of King Arthur (Aetas 60, 560, N.50). *Vide* later, pp. 151, 159.

13

West Hill Hill Hill. So that the explanation just offered of the name Glastonbury is not impossible. But quite different explanations are offered. A plausible one is set forth by Dr. C. R. Davey Biggs in his *Ictis and Avallon* (where he attempts to show that Avalon is also the celebrated Ictis), and he attributes all three names, Ynnis Witryn, Avalon, and Glastonbury as derivatives from persons all members of one ruling family. He derives the name Avalon from the King Avallach, Apallach, Aballac, Avalloc, of the Grail stories and early historians, the contemporary of St. Joseph; Witryn from Gwytherin, latinized as Victorinus, a descendant of Avallach; and Glastonbury from Glast, a contemporary of King Arthur, and another descendant of Avallach. Many others have derived Glastonbury from the borough of Glastings, the descendants of Glast. Be these theories as they may, "The Mother Church of the British Isles is the Church in Insula Avallonia, called by the Saxons 'Glaston'," wrote the learned Archbishop Ussher.

"It is certain that Britain received the Faith in the first age from the first sowers of the Word. Of all the churches whose origin I have investigated in Britain, the church of Glastonbury is the most ancient," wrote Sir Henry Spelman in his *Concilia*, and again he wrote in the same work: "We have abundant evidence that this Britain of ours received the Faith, and that from the disciples of Christ Himself, soon after the Crucifixion of Christ."[2]

Robert Parsons, the Jesuit, in his *Three Conversions of England*,[3] admits that "The Christian religion began in Britain within fifty years of Christ's ascension." His co-religionist, the very learned Alford, in his *Regia Fides*[4]

---

[2] Page 1 of the folio edition. See later.
[3] First under St. Joseph; second under Fagan and Dyfan; third under St. Augustine. Vol. 1, p. 26.
[4] Vol. 1, p. 19.

says: " It is perfectly certain that, before St. Paul had come to Rome, Aristobulus was absent in Britain."

The discreet Fuller goes so far as to say: " If credit be given to these ancient authors, this Church without competition was senior to all Christian Churches in the world."[5]

" Britain," wrote the erudite Polydore Vergil, " partly through Joseph of Arimathea, partly through Fugatus and Damianus, was of all kingdoms the first that received the Gospel."[6] Polydore Vergil had special access to sources of the Glastonbury story. He was Prebendary of Brent in Wells Cathedral, and Archdeacon of Wells, six miles from Glastonbury. In 1504 he was actually enthroned Bishop of Bath and Wells as proxy for his foreign non-resident kinsman, Adrian de Castello, and acted for him. He was very critical. He rejected the stories of Brute and Arthur, and despised Geoffrey of Monmouth. But he believed in the story of St. Joseph. He was a very liberal-minded man. In 1547 he signed a declaration in favour of the Communion in both kinds.[7] He was born at Urbino in Italy about 1470. He came of a literary family for four generations. One brother was a Professor of Philosophy at Pavia; another, Jerome, was a London merchant. He himself, after studying at Bologna and Padua, and acting as Chamberlain to Pope Alexander IV (1492-1498), came to England as Sub-Collector of Peter's Pence, and for some time he led a literary life in London, and Henry VII asked him to write an English History. Such was Polydore Vergil who bore the above testimony. The testimony of a learned Italian

[5] London edition, 1837. Vol. 1, Bk. 1, Sec. 13, p. 14.
[6] Lib. II.
[7] Forbidden in 1175: permitted by the Council of Basle 1431 onwards. This Council tried to establish that General Councils were above Popes. Eugenius IV had agreed but it deposed him.

steeped in English history, resident in England, well-versed
in the lore of Glastonbury, that England was the first
country to receive the Gospel is particularly valuable.

It is a matter of distinct interest, which we commend
to modern Roman Catholics, that Cardinal Pole, twice
over, when solemnly reconciling England to the Pope and
the Church of Rome, at the beginning of Queen Mary's
reign, claimed that Britain was the first country to be converted to Christianity. Before Philip and Mary under a
cloth of state, and the assembled Lords and Commons in
the great Chamber at Whitehall, the Cardinal said, "The
See Apostolic from whence I come hath a special respect
to this realm above all others, and not without cause, seeing
that God Himself, as it were, by providence hath given to
this realm prerogative of nobility above all others, which
to make plain unto you, it is to be considered that this
island first of all islands received the light of Christ's
religion", evidently confirming Gildas' statement![8]

The next day in Westminster Abbey, before Philip and
Mary in state, and the Lords and Commons assembled for
the act of reconciliation, the Cardinal uttered these words:
"Once again God hath given a token of His special favour
to the realm, for as this nation in the time of the Primitive
Church was the first to be called out of the darkness of
heathenism, so now they are the first to whom God has
given grace to repent of their schism," etc.[9] Too many
modern Catholics, and even modern Roman monks, are
much too fond of speaking as if all monks were liars and
inventors of fables. It does not increase one's respect for
modern monks. And it may be inconvenient, but in
passages like this Rome in her palmy days admitted that
the British Church was at least an elder sister, certainly not

[8] Fox's *Acts and Mon.*, Vol. VI, p. 568. *Chronicles of Queen
Jane*, Appendix X, pp. 154 and 13b.
[9] Fox's *Acts and Mon.*, Vol. VI, p. 572.

a daughter, of the Roman. Modern Roman Catholics are too often much more Roman than Catholic.

The Venerable Bede, writing about A.D. 740, says: "The Britons preserved the Faith which they had received under King Lucius uncorrupted, and continued in peace and tranquillity until the time of the Emperor Diocletian." That the Venerable Bede does not refer to St. Joseph is not surprising. Neither does he refer to St. Patrick. It may be pleaded that he was born and lived in the North. This would give more reason for his ignorance of St. Joseph than of St. Patrick, for the North owed so much to St. Patrick. Therefore the two silences rather drive us to Professor Stokes's explanation (*Ireland and the Celtic Church*, p. 29 note): "In presence of this notice [Cummian's reference to St. Patrick in A.D. 634 in his letter to the Abbot of Iona where he calls him 'St. Patrick, our Pope'] the silence of St. Bede about St. Patrick is of no account. He was intensely Roman, and despised the Celtic and Patrician party in England and Ireland alike." Bede's silence about St. Patrick must have been purposed. Very probably, therefore, that about St. Joseph was. And it helps us to realize how the memory of a great and flourishing Celtic Church was buried beneath the waves of heathen Saxon and Danish ravages, and the Romanizing Norman influence until it was revived in the reign of Henry II, by attention being drawn to Glastonbury and her two great stories by the discovery of the body of King Arthur.

Above are at random a number of quotations from recognized authorities of the immense antiquity and apostolic origin of our National Church, and of Glastonbury as being the Mother Church of the Island. It will be noticed that two distinct events are spoken of:

(1) The foundation of the Church in England by the Disciples of Christ.

(2) The acceptance of Christianity by the British Nation
     under Good King Lucius (Lleiver or Lleufer Mawr)
     about A.D. 170.

Britain was the first of all nations to accept Christianity
as its national religion. Few people realize that this is why
the British King is called " our Most Religious King ".

There remained for the French King the title of " Most
Christian King", and for the Spanish "Most Catholic
King ". We have too much forgotten our great inheritance,
which was so firmly defended by our British Archbishop
and Bishops in the days of St. Augustine.[10] How many
Britons realize that the superior dignity and antiquity of
our national Church has been decided by Church Councils?
It was never disputed till 1409 when, for political purposes,
it was called in question by the Ambassadors of France
and Spain, and then four times our claim was asserted at
the Councils of Pisa in 1409, Constance in 1417, Sienna in
1424, and Basle in 1434.[11] It was there contended that the
Churches of France and Spain must yield in points of
antiquity and precedence to that of Britain, as the latter
Church was founded by Joseph of Arimathea immediately
after the Passion of Christ ("statim post passionem
Christi "). There is a rare quarto giving the pleadings at
the Council of Constance.[12]

At Pisa in 1409 the English delegates were Robert
Hallam, Bishop of Salisbury, Henry Chichele (Archbishop

[10] Bede's *Ecc. Hist.* Bk. 2. Cap. 2, and Spelman's *Concilia*
p. 108.
[11] Nicholas Frome, Abbot of Glastonbury, was an English
envoy.
[12] *Disputatio super Dignitatem Angliae et Galliae in Concilio
Constantiano.* Theodore Martin, Lovan, 1517. This book was
printed through the influence of Sir Robert Wingfield, the
English ambassador to the Emperor Maximilian. (Cressy's
Church Hist. of Britain, Lib. II, p. 20.)

of Canterbury in 1414), and Thomas Chillenden, Prior of
Christ Church, Canterbury. Hallam was the leader. So
he was at Sienna in 1424. With him there was Nicholas
Bubwith, Bishop of Bath and Wells (whose chantry is in
the grave there), and the Bishop of St. David's. Cardinal
Beaufort, then Bishop of Winchester, joined them later.
He had been Dean of Wells. Evidently the authorities at
Wells, though there was constant friction between the
Abbots of Glastonbury and the Bishops of Bath and Wells,
believed in the claims of Glastonbury then. Nicholas
Frome, Abbot of Glastonbury, was actually one of the
English envoys at Basle in 1434. The Spanish Church
claimed to have been founded by St. James, the French by
Dionysius the Areopagite—hence St. Denis.

The learned Archbishop Ussher recording the claims
put forth by the English Church at these Councils specifically says that St. Joseph's burial at Glastonbury and the
donation of the XII Hides by King Arviragus to him was
the base of the claims.[13]

There are two different dates claimed for the founding
of Glastonbury Church, A.D. 37 and A.D. 63. Probably both
dates accentuate some special event. I will give one or two
reasons for the earlier date. Gildas the Wise, the earliest
Christian historian (A.D. 425–512) distinctly says that the
Light of Christ shone here in the last year of the reign of
Tiberius Caesar, that is A.D. 37. This falls in with the claim
recorded above, which gave precedence to British Bishops
at the Church Councils on the ground that Britain was
converted "immediately after the Passion of Jesus Christ".
It fits in also with the statements of Fuller and Polydore
Vergil already recorded (the latter a learned Italian) that

[13] Archbishop Ussher also refers to the two MS. transcripts
of the Council of Constance, one in the Royal Library, another
formerly the property of Cardinal Peter Bembi, in the private
library of D. Henry Wotton. Ussher, Cap. II.

the Church of Glastonbury was the Senior Church of the world; with Sir Henry Spelman's words that Britain received the Faith soon after the Crucifixion; with Alford's statement that Aristobulus was in Britain before St. Paul went to Rome; with the observance by the Greek Church of the martyrdom in Britain of Our Lord's disciple, St. Simon Zelotes, on May 10, A.D. 44 (a date supported by Cardinal Baronius); and with Hippolytus' (born about A.D. 160) inclusion of that Apostle in his list as "Bishop of the Britons". All these are testimony to the year A.D. 37 as marking the coming of the first Mission and not to the date A.D. 63.[14]

[14] It is quite possible that St. Joseph, familiar with Britain, brought the Blessed Virgin here as her Paranymphos when St. John was at Ephesus, A.D. 37, lived with her here till her *koimesis* fifteen years later, then went to France with St. Philip, was later sent by him to Britain as a missionary in A.D. 63. (See Pynson's *Metrical Life of St. Joseph*, A.D. 1520.)

PART II

TRADITIONS

St. Joseph of Arimathea
Good King Lucius
Our Lord and the Blessed Virgin
Topical Support of the Traditions

CHAPTER 2

ST. JOSEPH OF ARIMATHEA

IT is not too much to say that the site of St. Mary's Church in the Abbey grounds at Glastonbury is the site of the first known above-ground church in the world. The present ruined Norman church stands on the same site as the ancient Celtic wattle church which all tradition and history say was built by the Disciples of Christ. There was probably no other above-ground church in Rome than the Titulus till the time of Constantine the Great, when the Empire followed him in becoming Christian about A.D. 326. It is interesting to note the claim that this Titulus[1]—or Hospitium Apostolorum, or Palatium Britannicum—was the abode of Rufus Pudens, the Roman noble who married Claudia Britannica, the most cultured woman in Rome, apparently daughter of the British king, Caractacus, and sister of Linus, Bishop of Rome.[2] On the

[1] This " most ample house " with its baths named after Timothy and Novatus, two of the children of Rufus and Claudia, built on Viminalis Hill, became first a place where their daughter Praxedes hid martyrs, then a hospice for pilgrims from the East, and under Pope Evaristus (A.D. 100–109) a church, and was called Pastor's, probabiy after Pastor Hermas, who wrote to them. Baronius expressly calls St. Timothy a disciple of St. Peter and St. Paul (Vol. 2, Sec. 56, p. 47). Pastor Hermas says that all four children, Timotheus, Novatus, Praxedes, and Pudentiana, were instructed by preaching of the Apostles (Baronius, Vol. 2, Sec. 8–148.)

[2] Bishop, A.D. 69, martyred A.D. 90 (Baronius, Vol. 1, p. 778). In p. 739, he quotes Epiphanius as saying that SS. Peter and Paul were both Bishops in Rome (possibly the former presided over a Jewish, and the latter over a Gentile congregation) and that Linus succeeded them.

site of this house where St. Paul probably lived with the British Royal Family in exile, and from which he was probably martyred, is now a church dedicated to St. Puden-tiana, one of the martyred daughters of Pudens and Claudia. Pudens died, martyred, A.D. 96, and Claudia, who survived him one year, is said to have given the Titu-lus to be a Home for the Faithful, afterwards, between A.D. 100–109, to become a Christian church. This, as I shall show, is later than the date ascribed to the founding of St. Joseph of Arimathea's wattle church at Glaston-bury.[3]

It is not too much to say that the site of St. Mary's, Glastonbury, is the site of the earliest known above-ground church in the world. It is very interesting to note how the ancient British Royal Family was intimately connected with the earliest Apostolic Church, both in exile at Rome, and in Britain, where they fostered it. And there is a most interesting relic of the friendship of St. Paul and the Caractacus family in the existence of contemporary por-traits of St. Paul and Linus engraved in two glass paterae (in the Vatican Museum) depicted in Sir Wyke Bayliss's *Rex Regum* (pp. 60, 61). In the same Museum and the same book (pp. 73–75) there are contemporary portraits engraved on glass medallions with lines filled in with gold of (1) St. John, Damas, St. Peter, and St. Paul; (2) St. Peter and St. Paul; (3) Justin and St. Timothy, which makes all these people live to us.

---

[3] In the Glastonbury Museum, from the Glastonbury Lake Village about 100 B.C. can be seen remains of mud and wattle housing. W. M. Mackenzie in his *Pompeii* (Cap. 3, p. 41) writes : " The shepherds who came down from Alba Longa and founded Rome brought with them their type of dwelling-house of wood and wattled stubble which we see modelled in their burial urns." The Romans and the Britons claimed a common Trojan origin. Their facial resemblance is strong.

The Roman poet Martial shows that Claudia Rufina was British.[4] "Since Claudia wife of Rufus comes from the blue-set Britons, how is it that she has so won the hearts of the Latin people?" He praises her beauty and that of her three children as greater than that of Greeks and Italians. It is interesting that he speaks of Rufus as her "holy husband". In an earlier epigram he had written, "The foreign Claudia marries my Rufus Pudens." Martial was born in Bilbilis in Spain, and went to Rome A.D. 65. He wrote the above poem about A.D. 68. About the same time St. Paul links together the name of Pudens, Linus and Claudia with Eubulus in his greetings to St. Timothy from Rome (2 Tim. iv, 21). In Romans xvi, 13, he sends greetings from Corinth to "Rufus chosen in the Lord, and his mother, and mine", and in verse 10 he had sent greetings "to them which are of Aristobulus' household". I will hazard the guess that Aristobulus and Eubulus may be the same person. Eubulus means "prudent" or "well-counselling", and Aristobulus means "best counsellor". Eubulus may have been his right name, and Aristobulus a pet name, with a play upon the words. A Pudens, servant of the Emperor Claudius, is named among the sepulchral chambers of the Imperial household. It is a matter, too, of interest that the name of Pudens is also in the well-known Latin inscription on a stone discovered at Chichester, which narrates that Pudens, son of Pudentinus, gave a site there for a Temple to Neptune and Minerva. The inscription also bears the name of the Emperor Tiberius Claudius, who died in A.D. 37. This would be before the conversion of Rufus Pudens, and the dates fit in well. Baronius tells us that Rufus the Senator received St. Peter into his house on the Viminalis Hill in the year

[4] He calls her "Claudia peregrina et edita Britannis" (Martial, 13 B, XI, 53). (Foreign Claudia native of the Britons.)

A.D. 44.[5] He was apparently a Christian then, before receiving St. Peter. If he be the Pudens of the Chichester inscription he was apparently converted between these two dates.
Was Rufus Pudens, the Roman, converted in Britain? Was
it he who first brought Christianity into the British Royal
Family, when or before he married Gladys, soon by an
easy transition to become Claudia? It is a fascinating
question.

Cressy in his *Church History of Brittany*, 1618, tells us
"Our ancient histories report that Timotheus the eldest
son of Rufus came into Brittany [*sic*] where he converted
many to the faith, and at least disposed King Lucius to his
succeeding conversion." And Cardinal Baronius distinctly
says that Timotheus was a son of the most noble Roman
Senator, Rufus Pudens, a disciple of SS. Peter and Paul"
(Vol. 2, Sec. LVI, p. 47).

It seems that our early British Church was founded by
St. Joseph of Arimathea, that then St. Simon Zelotes the
Apostle came, and was martyred, and then St. Paul sent
Aristobulus, said to be the brother of St. Barnabas—and
thought by some to be of the family of Herod—to be our
first Bishop, and that he, too, was martyred. And I think
that it is indisputable that St. Paul himself came and
taught in Britain; and it is stated, but on less authority,
that St. Peter came.[6] Some think that as a result of these

---

[5] Baronius's *Annales*, Sec. 61, f.365. Those who wish to
study more closely the question of Rufus Pudens, Claudia,
Linus, St. Pudentiana, and St. Timothy, should refer to Ussher,
Brit. Eccl. Antiq., p. 19; Archdeacon Williams's *Claudia and
Pudens*; the Rev. R. W. Morgan's *St. Paul in Britain*, in which
the matter is fully treated; and Conybeare and Howson's *Life
and Epistles of St. Paul*, Vol. II, pp. 581, 582, 594, 595; and
Baronius's *Annales Ecclesiastic*, Vol. 1, p. 228, *re* Vol. 2, Sec.
56, p. 64; Secs. IV and V, pp. 111–112; Secs. I and II, pp. 148
and 150.

[6] The great rival abbeys and churches of Glastonbury and

early efforts, when Caractacus and his family went to Rome
as prisoners in A.D. 51, his sister Gladys, his daughters,
Gladys (who, in compliment to the Emperor Claudius is
said to have taken the name Claudia on her marriage to
Rufus Pudens), and Euergen,[7] and Linus his son were
already Christians; but Caractacus and his aged father
Bran,[8] who had become an Arch-Druid, were unconverted,
probably through troubles of State and war. The Welsh
Triads say that Bran was baptized in Rome in A.D. 58 by
St. Paul.[9] When they came back they were Christians, and
thenceforth fostered and protected in Siluria or South
Wales the Christian Church. Bran returned to Britain
before Caractacus, A.D. 58, very probably as a missionary.

Bran Vendigaid, or the Blessed, was a very remarkable
personality. The Welsh Triads not only speak of him as
one of the introducers of Christianity,[10] but together

Westminster were both dedicated to St. Peter and St. Paul.
The one at Glastonbury was built on to the east end of St.
Mary's, the Olde Churche. One was the Church of the Celtic
and the early Saxon dynasties, the other of the later Saxon.

[7] St. Eurgen of Caer Salog (Salisbury) and of Llan Ilid,
Glamorganshire, was the first British female saint.

[8] That Tacitus does not mention Bran being taken prisoner
is not a great obstacle. He may have been, but unknown to
him, or Bran may well have joined his son, after the latter was
given his life, and freedom to live in Rome.

[9] Bp. Edwards of St. Asaph's *Landmarks in the history of
the Welsh Church*, p. 2. The date given by the Triads is
impossible. St. Paul did not go to Rome till A.D. 62. The date
58 is probably the date of the baptism, and the Apostle's name
an addition. The Triads hail from the book of Caradoc of
Llancarvan, who died in 1156, but most of the events in them
refer to the 6th century. And some must be older than that,
e.g. one speaks of Glastonbury, Llan Iltud and Ambresbury
as the three principal Choirs of Britain, but Ambresbury fell
in the 6th century.

[10] Triads, 18 and 35, 3rd Series. *Myvyrian Arch.*, Vol. 2.

with Prydain and Dyfnwal as the three who consolidated elective monarchy in Britain. The Triads call the descendants of Bran one of the Three Holy Families of Britain.[11]

All the earliest traditions of Glastonbury circle round St. Joseph. Its name, the Secret of the Lord, probably comes from his having buried the Holy Grail there, and his being buried there with the two phials with the Blood and Sweat of our Lord.[12] The Church of St. Mary on the site of the ancient wattle church is ever locally called " St. Joseph's Chapel ". Tradition still shows there Wyrrall or Weary All Hill, on which St. Joseph and his eleven tired companions are said to have rested on their first landing, for Glastonbury was an island in those days.

It is generally assumed that St. Joseph arrived at Weary All by water. But it would have been probably equally possible for him to have arrived there at low tide on foot by the ancient Causeway from Street, crossing the Brue by the Pons Perilous, or Pomparles Bridge, from which some five centuries later King Arthur is said to have thrown away his famous sword Excalibur, forged at Glastonbury. The only link which suggests arriving from the mainland

[11] Bran is stated to have returned mortally wounded from his punitive expedition to Ireland, and ordered his companions to carry his head to be buried in the White Hill, London (where the White Tower now stands), as a protection against future invasions, and there it remained till, some 500 years later, King Arthur had it removed. *Vide Mabinogion.* The *Mabinogion* (the plural of Mabinogi) are the oldest remains of Welsh mythological sagas. Every young Bard had to learn them by heart, which confirms Caesar's statement that the Druids never committed their learning to writing, although it is said that they used Greek letters in writing.

[12] For the story of his bringing the two phials *vide* p. 94. The Holy Grail is supposed to have been buried near Chalice Well, on Chalice Hill, whence their name. For the name " Secret of the Lord," *vide* later.

is a lingering tradition that St. Joseph founded a cell at
Crewkerne on his way to Glastonbury. Of course that may
have been on some return journey from or to Glastonbury
some years later. The founding of a cell suggests this.
Some hermit may have settled there. Very probably a
very ancient figure with a staff on the outside of Crewkerne Church, which probably came from an earlier
church than the beautiful Gothic one there now, may be
that of St. Joseph. The late Alderman John Morland, of
Glastonbury, a very sound antiquary, found a corduroy
road, at least as old as the Romans, parallel to the present
road from Street. But besides the possibility of arriving at
Weary All direct by water, or coming on foot from the
mainland, there is yet another possible theory full of
interest and romance. The antiquary Eyston, in 1714, in
*A little Monument to the once famous Abbey and Borough
of Glastonbury*, published by Hearne in 1722, narrates
some traditions (some rather vague and inaccurate) which
he had gathered from the landlord of an inn, probably the
"Pilgrims' Inn" or "George", who rented a large part of
the Abbey enclosure. One of these traditions was "that
St. Joseph of Arimathea landed not far from the town, at
a place where there was an oak planted in memory of his
landing, called ' The Oak of Avalon '; that he and his companions marched thence to a Hill, near a mile on the south
side of the Town, and there being weary rested themselves,
which gave the Hill the name of Wearyall Hill; that St.
Joseph stuck on the Hill his staff, being a dry hawthorn
stick, which grew, and constantly budded and blowed upon
Christmas Day." The mere mention of "The Oak of
Avalon" awakens the deepest interest. There still linger
two ancient trees called "The Oaks of Avalon". They are
also called Gog and Magog.

They are almost the last remains of an ancient Druidic
grove at the foot of Stonedown (a name which bespeaks

its Druidic use).[13] From them ran also an avenue of oaks which led towards the Tor. This grove and avenue were shamefully cut down about 1906 to clear the ground of a farm! The trees were immense. They were all sold to Messrs. J. Snow & Son, timber merchants of Glastonbury. Mr. Curtis of that firm remembers five boys standing in one of them called Magog when he was a boy. The real Magog was cut down and so probably was the real Gog. Magog was eleven feet in diameter, and more than 2,000 season-rings were counted. Besides the two trees still called Gog and Magog, there are, by an ancient narrow road, now a lane, the remains of five other immense oaks. The biggest of all (possibly the real Gog) is cut down and prone on its side, and looks from the road across a field something like a shed. In hedges there are two other giants just dragging out the last flicker of life, and there are fragments of two other dead monarchs (doubtless some of those that were cut down) in hedges. From the real Magog Mr. James, a late member of the firm, many years ago made a Glaston-

[13] The dolmens and menhirs have long disappeared. Stones may be buried. More likely they have been used for building and road-mending. The writer always suspects that the church on the Tor was built of Druidic stones to assert the victory of Christ and Christianity on the site of the old religion. Near the age-long pilgrim path up the Tor there still linger three stones, very probably the remains of a menhir or stone table. Dr. Davey Biggs, in *Ictis and Avallon* points out how the Iberian metal-seekers built these stone monuments. If St. Joseph did land at this grove, the tradition that St. Paul landed at Paul's Grove near Porchester is of great interest. That tradition should have linked the landing place of both these traditional missionaries with groves is startling, the more so as the habit of planting trees to commemorate important visits still lingers. Rutter in his *North-West Somerset*, 1829, p. 87, in a footnote, gives a very unusual derivation of the name Glastonbury, as Glastan-byrie, the Hill of Oaks, which is interesting.

bury chair, candlesticks, bowls and picture frames, as a
hobby. The oak is extraordinarily red, and of an unique
grain or "figure".

In 1935, Mr. Ackroyd Gibson of Glastonbury profession-
ally made many bowls out of the remains of these trees.
The Oaks of Avalon were there when St. Joseph came, but
one may have been planted later to commemorate his coming. More likely the tradition is slightly jumbled, but it is
not altogether to be despised. The Oaks of Avalon are to
the north-east of the Tor. The sea must have come up to
just below the oaks, and it would have been a very possible
landing place, and the ancient hill-road Paradise Lane, to
the north of the Tor, leads to Weary-All, joining the
ancient road from Wells. They would pass a dell now
called "Paradise" (vide p. 54), in spring a haunt of prim-
roses. The ordnance map shows a footpath from Paradise
Lane down to the Oaks of Avalon which has lately got
obscured at its latter end. Both the roadways and the foot-
paths to these historic Oaks of Avalon ought to be
improved and marked by sign-posts. The view across the
Vale of Avalon by the footpath is beautiful in the extreme.
The very names Gog and Magog are arresting. Nennius in
his *History of the Britons*, A.D. 796, edited in the 10th century by Mark the Hermit, tells us that Magog was the
second son of Japhet the son of Noah. Quite likely Gog
is the shortening of the name Gomer. Gomer, from whom
came the Gomeri or Cwmri (Cymri), the forefathers of the
British, who was the eldest-born of Japhet. It was because
the Cymri were the eldest-born of the tribes of Japhet, that
the Arch-druid was found in this Island, and not on the
Continent. We read that when Brute, from whom Britain
takes its name, came here about 1130 B.C., he and his people
drove the "Giants" into mountain caves, and so on. His
companion, Corineus, struggled with and slew a monster,
Goemagot, said to be twelve cubits high, who could pull up

an oak in one shake, and who inhabited the west country
(*Geoffrey of Monmouth*, Bk. 1, cap. 16). Brute, the fore-
father of the British Kings, was stated to be the descendant of Aeneas of Troy. According to the *Receuill des
Histoires de Troye*, Gog and Magog, two giants, were
brought to London (Troia Nova, hence Trinobantes) by
Brute and his companions. Hence the old statues of Gog
and Magog in the Guildhall, London. Gog and Magog
figure in Ezekiel (cap. 38 and 39) and the Revelations (cap.
20) as evil powers. The name lingers in the Gogmagog
hills in Cambridgeshire where there is a camp of thirteen
acres with triple defences. There are remains of earth-
works near Gog and Magog in Avalon. There are still two
great oak trees in Yardley Chase in Northamptonshire
called Gog and Magog which were depicted in Strutt's *Sylva
Britannica* in 1830. The names seem connected with great
antiquity, powers of evil, struggles, hills, and oaks.

We can tell by their season-rings that the Oaks of
Avalon, remains of seven of which still linger, were here
when St. Joseph came, and it is extremely possible that he
landed there,[14] and proceeded past Paradise and the Tor to
rest on Wirral (through tradition to be called Weary-All)
and plant his staff there. There the King Arviragus met
him and made his donation of land. Both Arviragus and
the Druids may have known St. Joseph as a trader and
metal merchant before he came here as a missionary. On
Wearyall there grew the famous Holy Thorn (*Crataegus
monogyna praecox*), which is said to have sprung from his
staff which he planted in the fertile ground, possibly as a
token of taking possession of the XII Hides of land[15]

[14] They are about sea-level.
[15] The exact size of a Hide is uncertain. It was a portion of
land, variable in extent, but sufficient to support one family.
Coke lays it down that its number of acres was indeterminate.
Eight hides composed " a Knight's Fee ". But the *Liber de*

which King Arviragus,[16] cousin of Caractacus, granted to him and his followers, much as to-day we plant a flag-staff and a Union Jack on taking over new territory. This tree, a branch of which, in flower, was always sent to the King on old Christmas Day, at any rate as late as the reign of Charles I—a custom happily revived in the last few years—survived the Reformation.[17] Its claims to sanctity awakened the ire of an unhappy Puritan, who expressed himself by diligently and impiously trying to cut it down. It was a gigantic tree for a thorn, and was in two parts. One part he demolished, the other he wounded mortally. And then it revenged itself. A splinter from it flew into his eye

---

Soliaco (temp. Rich. I) tells us that at Glastonbury itself I hide (16 furlongs)= 160 acres, and one Knight's Fee or 4 hides =640 acres. In Canada to-day, a township consists of 36 sections of 640 acres or 1 square mile each, and sections are divided into quarter-sections of 160 acres each, an interesting survival. Ultimately Glaston XII Hides was the name of a district several miles in extent over which the Abbot had supreme jurisdiction, even to the power of life and death. The old title apparently remained when there were many more than XII Hides. The Abbey also held much property outside its juris-diction.

[16] Juvenal in a Satire makes one of his characters ask a pale, nervous-looking man: "What is the matter with you? Have you seen the car-driven British King, Arviragus?" Pitsaeus (Pitts), the Continental Roman Canon, 1619, in his *Hist. de Rebus Anglicis* includes King Arviragus as "illustrious writer of Britain", refers to his wife Genuissa (said to be a daughter of the Emperor Claudius), and speaks of a letter to his cousin Caractacus, another to Leaders, Cotredus, and Comus, and one "ad suos proceres".

[17] Pere Cyprian Gamache, Roman Catholic Confessor to Queen Henrietta Maria, tells how Charles I chaffed him because the miraculous tree contradicted the Pope by blossom-ing on old Christmas Day and not on new (Agnes Strickland's *Lives of the Queens of England*, Vol. 5, p. 437, and Coulburn's *Court and Times of Charles I*, Vol. 2, p. 417).

and finished him. The wounded tree itself lingered some thirty years—in fact, saw a generation come which hated and revolted from the Puritans—and then died. But in the meantime various thorns were budded from it. One is in the Abbey grounds, a better one in the parish church-yard, and a still better one in the vicarage garden. There are others in various parts. It cannot be struck, but can be budded. It seems to be a Levantine thorn. Most botanists agree to this. Certain it is that, in addition to flowering profusely in May, it keeps the habit of blossoming again at Christmastide, but more freely on old Christmas Day. And nearly always on Christmas Day flowers from it are placed on the altar of the glorious parish church of St. John the Baptist.

CHAPTER 3

GOOD KING LUCIUS

ST. JOSEPH's little circle of twelve disciples was kept going
by anchorites—as one died another was appointed; but in
course of time a certain slackness seems to have come over
them. William of Malmesbury tells us that the holy spot
at length became a covert of wild beasts.[1] Then in the
days of Good King Lucius aforesaid came a revival.
Llewrug Mawr, Llewrug the Great (grandson of Saint
Cyllinus[2] and great-grandson of Caractacus), nicknamed
Lleiver Mawr or the great luminary (hence his Latinized
name of Lux or Lucius), was king in Britain in the middle
and towards the end of the 2nd century. He increased the
Light that the first missionaries, the disciples of Christ,
had brought, by sending emissaries to Eleutherius, Bishop
of Rome, requesting him to send missionaries to Britain.
The Welsh Triads tell us that Eleutherius, in response, sent
Dyfan and Fagan, Medwy and Elfan,[3] all of them British

[1] Cap. I.

[2] It is interesting that in Cyllinus's reign the Cymry babies
first received names—Christian baptism. Gwehelyth Jestyn ap
Gwrgant.

[3] Monkish historians say that Elfan was the second Bishop
of London. (Theanus, who died A.D. 185, was the first Bishop
of London.) The Latin Book of Llandaff says that he was
consecrated Bishop at the time of his mission to Rome. Welsh
authorities say that he presided over a congregation of Christians at Glastonbury (*vide* Rev. Rice Rees's *Lives of Welsh
Saints*). Godwin (*de Præsulibus*, pp. 169–170) says that he was
brought up at Glastonbury, and was sent by Lucius to Eleutherius, that he founded a library "near the aforesaid Church"
(St. Peter's, Cornhill, which was his seat as Bishop of London),

names, in A.D. 167. But John Harding, in the reign of
Edward IV, puts their mission at A.D. 190, which fits in
with the papacy of Eleutherius, as does the date 183 given
by Cardinal Baronius.

Geoffrey of Monmouth tells us that Gildas (A.D. 516–570)
recorded the names and acts of these missionaries in a book
now lost, *The Victory of Aurelius Ambrosius.*[4]

The story appears again in the second revision of the
Liber Pontificalis about A.D. 685. The Venerable Bede, A.D.
673–735, tells the story of Lucius's appeal to Eleutherius.
But we hear little or nothing of the appeal to Rome until
after the Augustinian Italian mission to this country in
597. The Latin Book of Llandaff, or Book of Teilo (probably compiled by Bishop Urban in the 12th century, but
based upon a book of Bishop Teilo, A.D. 540), and John of
Teignmouth in his life of St. Dubricius (A.D. 1346), and
Capgrave (A.D. 1393–1464),[5] "the most learned of English
Augustinians whom the soil of England ever produced",
and Archbishop Ussher in his *De Brittanicarum Ecclesi-
arum Primordiis* (pp. 49–50) tell us that Medwy and Elfan

---

and that he converted many Druids. Pitsaeus, the aforesaid
Roman Catholic Canon in his *Relationes Historicæ de Rebus
Anglicis* (Paris, 1619), among many "illustrious British
writers" names Elvanus of Avalon, whom he puts about
A.D. 180, and says that he was educated in the School of St.
Joseph of Arimathea, and that he wrote "concerning the
origin of the British Church".

[4] For Aurelius Ambrosius as a real historical person of
importance, *vide* W. A. S. Hewins's *The Royal Saints of
Britain*, pp. 9 and 52–56.

[5] *Nat. Dic. Biog.* John Capgrave was Provincial of his order,
Augustinian Friars in England and received Henry VI at his
Friary in Lynn in 1446. He was born in 1393, and a Priest in
1417–18. He quotes a book said to have been found by the
Emperor Theodisius in Pilate's Pretorium at Jerusalem, relat-
ing to St. Joseph of Arimathea.

were Britons who were sent as emissaries by Good King
Lucius and returned with the missionaries Dyfan and
Fagan. It is noticeable that the pedigree of Dyfan, as given
in the Cambrian Biography, makes him a Briton. The
pedigree may be spurious, or he may have been a Briton
resident in Rome. William of Malmesbury calls them
Fagan and Deruvian, and Geoffrey of Monmouth Faganus
and Duvanus. These missionaries journeyed through
Britain and came to Glastonbury. "There, God leading
them," wrote William of Malmesbury, "they found an
old church built, as 'twas said, by the hands of Christ's
disciples, and prepared by God Himself for the salvation
of souls, which Church the Heavenly Builder Himself
showed to be consecrated by many miraculous deeds, and
many Mysteries of healing. . . . And they afterwards pon-
dered the Heavenly message that the Lord had specially
chosen this spot before all the rest of Britain as the place
where His Mother's name might be invoked. They also
found the whole story in ancient writings, how the Holy
Apostles, having been scattered throughout the world, St.
Philip coming into France with a host of disciples sent
twelve of them into Britain to preach, and that there,
taught by revelation they constructed the said chapel which
the Son of God afterwards dedicated to the honour of His
Mother; and, that to these same twelve, three kings, pagan
though they were, gave twelve portions of land for their
sustenance. Moreover, they found a written record of their
doings, and on that account they loved this spot above all
others, and they also, in memory of the first twelve, chose
twelve of their own, and made them live on the island
with the approval of King Lucius. These twelve thereafter
abode there in divers spots as anchorites—in the same
spots, indeed, which the first twelve inhabited [tradition-
ally in huts round the wonderful Chalice Well at the foot
of St. Michael's Tor]. Yet they used to meet together con-

tinuously in the Old Church in order to celebrate Divine
worship more devoutly, just as the three pagan kings had
long ago granted the said island with its surroundings to
the twelve former disciples of Christ, so the said Phagan
and Deruvian [Dyfan] obtained it from King Lucius for
these their twelve companions and for others to follow
thereafter. And thus, many succeeding these, but always
twelve in number, abode in the said island during many
years up to the coming of St. Patrick, the apostle of the
Irish."[6]

Fox, in his *Acts and Monuments* (Vol. 1, p. 146), gives
Eleutherius's letter to King Lucius, in reply to his request.
It runs thus: " Ye require of us the Roman laws, and the
Emperor's to be sent over to you, which you may practice
and put in use in your realm. The Roman laws and the
Emperor's we may ever reprove, but the law of God we
may not. Ye have received of late through God's mercy
in the realm of Britain the Law and Faith of Christ. Ye
have with you within the realm both the parties of the
Scriptures. Out of them, by God's grace, with the council
of your realm, take ye a law that can (through God's
sufferance) rule your kingdom of Britain. For ye be God's
Vicar in your kingdom, according to the saying of the
Psalm, 'O God, give Thy judgment to the King,' etc."
In the margin, Fox has this note: " Ex vetusto codice

---

[6] William of Malmesbury's *Antiquities of Glastonbury*, cap.
2. Those who have contended that there is no earlier authority
than William of Malmesbury for the Great St. Patrick being
first Abbot and dying at Glastonbury are upset by the discovery, in 1924, of St. Dunstan's own Psalter which he used
at Canterbury, in the Calendar attached to which we read of
" St. Patrick Senior at Glaston," *vide* Dean Armitage Robinson's *Times of St. Dunstan*, p. 100. This is some 150 years
earlier than William of Malmesbury. It is very significant that
Irish pilgrims haunted Glastonbury in the Middle Ages. But
see later, pp. 45–47, 77.

regum antiquorum "—from an old writing of ancient Kings.

Good King Lucius probably flourished about the middle of the 2nd century: the Latins said in the latter part, the Welsh said in the middle. Probably both are right, as the time fits in well with the reigns of the two Antonines, whose edicts favoured the Christians, and the date of the Embassy to Eleutherius is probably A.D. 183. In his time Britain, first of all countries, became Christian. Hence the proud title of our Kings " Most Religious King "—just as from St. Joseph came the precedence of British Bishops. The Welsh Triads tell us that Lucius " bestowed the free-dom of the country and nation with the privilege of judg-ment and surety, upon those who might be in the faith of Christ."[7] Cressy, the Benedictine monk, who lived shortly after the Reformation, and who had imbibed many of the traditions of the Benedictine Monastery of Glaston-bury[8] kept alive on the Continent, tells us in his *Church History of Brittany* that, in company with his sister, St. Emerita, King Lucius finally went as a missionary through Bavaria, Rhoetia, and Vindelicia, and was martyred near Curia, in Germany.[9]

Some, who have studied the subject of Good King Lucius, claim that he died a Confessor in the City of Gloucester, and was buried in the Church of St. Mary de Lode there. They claim that the Roman Martyrology has confused the British with the Bavarian Lucius. Among those who think so is Monsignor Bernard Williams of

[7] Triad 35, 3rd Series.

[8] He mentions that St. Joseph died at Glastonbury on July 27, A.D. 82.

[9] The story of Good King Lucius appears in writing as early as the second revision of the *Liber Pontificalis* about A.D. 685. At Chur (Coire) the capital of the Grisons Canton, Switzerland, they state that Lucius King of the British and his sister are buried in the crypt of the very interesting old cathedral there.

Painswick, Gloucestershire. The tradition is that Lucius built the Church of St. Mary de Lode in Gloucester. It is worth remembering that the learned Fox in his *Acts and Monuments*, Vol. 1, p. 147, wrote: " The said Lucius after he had founded many churches, and given great riches and liberties to the same, deceased with great tranquillity in his own land, and was buried at Gloucester the 14th year after his baptism, as the book *Flores Historiarum* doth count, which was the year of Our Lord (as he saith) 201, and reckoneth his conversion to be Anno 187. In some I find his decease to be the 4th and in some the 10th year after his baptism, and hold that he reigned in all the space of 77 years." We must not forget that the Abbey of Westminster, then the Isle of Thorney, included good King Lucius in her claims.

The Most Rev. Bernard Mary Williams, Roman Catholic Archbishop in England (pro-Uniate Rite), has lent me his MS. notes on King Lucius, many of which I cite or quote here.[10] The Archbishop calls his notes rough MS. notes on " Lucius first Christian King of Britain ". He cites an English abridgment (1718) of Sir William Dugdale's *Monasticon Anglicanum* as saying, " There is a tradition that a Bishop and Preachers were settled at Gloucester immediately after Lucius the first Christian King of Britain embraced the Faith, that is in the year of Grace 189. Antiquity testified that Eldadryn was Bishop of Gloucester in 489, and Dubricius in 522. Nay, the ancients make Gloucester an Arch-episcopal See, when Lucius by the advice of Fugacius and Damianus sent hither by Pope Eleutherius converted the three Archflamens of London, York, and Gloucester into so many Archbishoprics. Afterwards the See was translated to Menevia or St. David's

[10]I also am extremely indebted to Mrs. Doughty, wife of the late Vicar of St. Peter's, Cornhill, for much of the information which I give here about that church.

in Wales, but in the year 679 Wolphen the first Christian King of the Mercians beautified and enlarged Gloucester."

The Monsignor points out that the Book of Llandaff (see p. 130) tells of Lucius' embassy of Elfan and Medwy to Eleutherius and gives the date as 156, and it says that "Elfan was ordained a Bishop, and Medwy a Doctor". He says that "it was from Glastonbury that King Lucius first heard of the Christian Faith". He also tells that "King Lucius' embassy is mentioned in the *Chronicle of Fabius Ethelwerd*, A.D. 975–1011, in the *Anglo-Saxon Chronicle* most likely written by King Alfred the Great, or at any rate up to A.D. 891 or so, and in Bede's *Ecclesiastical History*, A.D. 730. All these I have verified. None of these mentions St. Joseph of Arimathea, or the first beginnings at Glastonbury, and this for two reasons: (1) they were of different race and unfriendly; (2) they all wrote after the coming of St. Augustine, A.D. 597, and were unwilling to mention a British Catholic Foundation older than Rome itself." It is interesting that the Archbishop, a strong champion of the Papacy, and myself, have separately arrived at these two reasons.

He tells in his Notes, and in letters to me, that King Lucius built four churches in the following order (omitting St. Michael's on Glastonbury Tor, which was probably the first, as Lucius was baptized in the Chalice Well at the foot of the Tor): first, St. Mary ad Portam, now St. Mary de Lode, in this capital city of Caer-Glow (Gloucester); second, the first Church at Llandaff; third, the first Church at Winchester; and, fourth, St. Peter's, Cornhill. St. Mary de Lode apparently remained the only church in Gloucester till Wolphen laid the foundations of his abbey, the first abbey there. The abbey in course of time became the present cathedral. But he says that St. Mary de Lode " was undoubtedly the Cathedral of the Archdiocese [of Glou-

cester] from the time of Lucius until the See was translated
to Menevia, otherwise St. David's. There are grounds for
believing that Caer Glow remained an Episcopal See,
possibly of reduced dignity, until Saxon times, when it
became part of the Diocese of Worcester."

The Archbishop mentions that the learned Alban Butler
(A.D. 1710–1773) says that the fact that Lucius was a
Christian King in Britain is proved by two medals mentioned by Ussher (*Antiq. Brit.*, c. 3) and one by Bouterus.
Butler says that the two British coins of Lucius bear with
the word "Luc." the figure of the Cross. This is over a
century before Constantine the Great, and contradicts the
theory that no coin bore that emblem before Constantine.
He also says that King Lucius was first buried at St. Mary
de Lode, Gloucester, then translated "to St. Peter's, Cornhill, as set forth in an inscription formerly found there.
Later still the body was brought back to Gloucester,
probably by the Earls of Berkeley or the Cliffords, or both,
and reburied in the Choir of the Franciscan Church, which
these great families founded." He goes on to say that much
of the Church of the Grey Friars remains, and part of it is or
was in the occupation of Mr. W. Bayley, a wine merchant.
"The Choir, however, is wholly destroyed and the portion
in which the King's body still rests is almost certainly
beneath Suffolk House. There are also the bodies of a
Countess of Berkeley, murdered at Gloucester, and a
Bishop of Worcester who resigned and became a Franciscan. There is a quotation of the inscription formerly in
St. Peter's, Cornhill, in *A Guide to the Cathedral* (Gloucester) published in 1867 by the Rev. H. Haines, only two
copies of which are known to exist. I have seen one of
these. This mentions the burial of the King in London,
and later the re-burial in the Grey Friars at Gloucester,
quoting an authority in 1641. King Lucius was baptized
on May 28, and died on December 3, 201. His feast has

been kept on both these days, but the latter is now universal."[11]

Most of the following about St. Peter's, Cornhill, comes from Mrs. Doughty aforesaid. There is today in the Vestry of St. Peter's, Cornhill, a plate claiming that it is the oldest Church foundation in London and founded by Good King Lucius. The present plate was put up after the Great Fire of London in 1666, the older one having been destroyed by the fire. It is a partly modernized translation of the old one. The latter can be seen in Weaver's *Funeral Monuments*, 1637. It was also given by Archbishop Ussher in 1639, by Stow in 1598, and Holinshed in 1577. It refers to the Franciscan House in Gloucester which was not founded till 1268, so that the tablet cannot be older than that. Ralph de Baldoc, Bishop of London in 1304, speaks of a copy of it being hung in the Vestry of old St. Paul's Cathedral. As he died in 1313, the tablet cannot be later. St. Peter's, Cornhill, was the first church of the Bishops of London. There can be little reasonable doubt that this ancient story of its being founded by Lucius is true. I may mention that Geoffrey of Monmouth, Bk. 4. Cap. XIX, tells that the Druidical Flamens became Bishops, and the Archflamens, Archbishops. These Archbishops are generally supposed to be London, York, and Caerleon on Usk. The City of Legions is the name given for the latter. Archbishop Williams has shown that he and Dugdale think that the third was Gloucester. Anyway, the claim in olden days led to serious trouble between Canterbury, London and York. Geoffrey of Monmouth distinctly says that the City of Legions was the third Archbishopric, and that it was situated on the River Usk in Glamorganshire. He also says

---

[11] The Archbishop gives as his references Ussher *Brit.*, c.3; Stillingfleet orig., c.II; Selden *Analect Anglo-Britan*, C.6.2, p. 895; Alford *Annal. Brit. ad. an.*, 182; *Baronius ad. an.*, 183; Collier *Hist. Sec. Brit.*, c.I; Tillemont, t.3, pp. 62 and 615.

that the Bishops under these three were twenty-eight in number.

Nothing perhaps is more revealing of the way in which the history of our Celtic Church has been forgotten than this story about good King Lucius. The man in the street knows nothing about him. But Bede, Nennius, the Book of Llandaff, the Welsh Triads, the Mabinogion, Achaury Saint, Geoffrey of Monmouth, William of Malmesbury, Cressy, Cardinal Baronius, Ussher, and Rees, have told of him. Ussher in particular has written long and fully, in chapters III–IV. The very uncertainty of the exact date of his conversion tells the same tale. Ussher quotes twenty-three of them and then decides on A.D. 176 himself; Bede says A.D. 180; Nennius says A.D. 164; the Welsh Triads, the middle of the 2nd century; Malmesbury, A.D. 167; and the learned Cardinal Baronius, A.D. 183. If it took place in the papacy of Eleutherius, this latter date is more likely. The catalogue of the Ancient Bishops of Rome originally only gave the name of the Pontiffs and the length of their reign. This was written shortly after A.D. 353, but as early as about A.D. 530 an interpolated copy has the words in Latin under Eleutherius's name: "he receives a letter from Lucius, King of Britain, that he might be made a Christian by his command". So the story was told then. Malmesbury in 1135 says A.D. 167, which cuts out Eleutherius, and Nennius says 164, which does the same. But there is a great volume of tradition which recounts the Baptism of Lucius, and the early national conversion of Britain. St. Peter's, Cornhill, in London, proclaims it, so do the early centres of British Christianity, Glastonbury, Llandaff, and Gloucester. And the story lingers in the name of the following churches (three in Glamorganshire): Llanfedwy (Medwy's Church); Merthyr Dyfan (Dyfan the Martyr); St. Fagan's; and Llan-Lleirwg (Lleirwg's or Lucius' Church), now St. Mellon's, near Cardiff.

Just as it is very suspect whether the claim that Pope
Celestine sent St. Patrick to Ireland be not a claim of after
centuries, so a typical claim about Eleutherius may have
crept into the Good King Lucius story. It may be true.
The story, as it is told, suggests that Lucius, great-grandson
of Arviragus, before he quite embraced the Christian
religion, sent messengers to Rome, the centre of civiliza-
tion. But the case of St. Patrick makes us suspicious. St.
Patrick's name was Succat. The name Patricius or Patrick
was used as late as the 7th century to denote gentle or
noble birth.

William of Malmesbury tells us (in Cap. 8) that St.
Patrick was the first to gather the Anchorites at Glastonbury, unbroken successors of St. Joseph and his eleven
companions, under one roof. It has often been contended
that the Glastonbury St. Patrick was not the Apostle of
Ireland. We have pointed out the evidence of the calendar
attached to the Bosworth Psalter supporting the claim in
St. Dunstan's time. But there is evidence practically contemporary with St. Patrick, that the great St. Patrick died
and was buried at Glastonbury. It is very likely that he was
born and brought up in the neighbourhood. His father
was Calpurnius, a deacon; his mother was Concessa; his
grandfather was Potitus, a priest and also a *decimo* or
magistrate of a Romano-British colony; and his great-
grandfather was Odissus, another deacon—a name
strangely recalling the wily Odysseus of Homer. So he
lived in some Church centre. He tells us that he was born
near Nem Thor, which means the lofty hill or tor. Another
name connected with his birth was Bannavem Taberniae.
I hazarded the guess that this was a corruption of the
name Bona Venta Hiberniæ, good market or meeting place
for Ireland. Dr. Davey Biggs of Oxford arrived indepen-
dently at the conclusion that the first part was Bona Venta,
a Venta being a well-known centre. I think that this may

have been Bristol, 27 miles from Glastonbury. The Irish
frequently raided the neighbourhood of Bristol, and Irish
raiders carried St. Patrick as a prisoner to Ireland for six
years. Be this as it may, there is the ancient evidence in
the text of this book for the great St. Patrick being buried
at Glastonbury.

St. Patrick being a Briton, it was quite natural for him to
return to his native country, and quite natural to choose
Glastonbury, the great Church centre there, and possibly
his birthplace.

It is very suspect whether the claim that Pope Celestine
sent St. Patrick to Ireland be not a claim of after centuries.
St. Patrick was the nephew maternally of the French
Bishop St. Martin of Tours. A marginal note in the
Cambridge MS. of William of Malmesbury's *De Antiquitate Glastoniae* tells us that St. Patrick after his captivity
in Ireland met in England the two French Bishops St.
Germanus and St. Lupus (after the Alleluia victory) and
that he was twenty-two years under the teaching of St.
Germanus at Auxerre. The honest and learned Abbé
Riguet says that Pope Celestine consecrated St. Palladius
instead of St. Patrick. He says " some authors, anxious to
connect the Church of Ireland with Rome, wish to say that
the Apostle was ordained Bishop by Pope Celestine. This
is a detail which older documents do not give. . . . The first
Bishop of Ireland is certainly Palladius, and not Patrick.
On hearing of the death of Palladius, Patrick retraced his
steps to Auxerre, where he was ordained by St. Germanus."

Furthermore, Bede, so devoted to Rome, never even
mentions St. Patrick! He ignores the Celtic saint consecrated by a French Bishop!

The marginal note above referred to is only more explicit
in detail than Malmesbury is in the text, for there he says
that at the time of troubles with the Angles and the Pelagian heretics St. Germanus of Auxerre came to the help

of the British, winning the Alleluia Victory, and returning home " took Patrick into the company of his immediate followers, and sent him some years afterwards by the command of Pope Celestine to preach to the Irish." But there is very little doubt that, although Rome and the Celtic Church were quite friendly in those days, Germanus acted on his own initiative. This accounts for the silence of Bede about Patrick. Bede's interests and knowledge were wrapped up mainly in the Roman Church and not in the great missionary efforts of the Celtic Church.

On the other hand, the remains of dedications of the above churches to Medwy, Lucius' messenger, and Dyfan and Fagan, the Pope's messengers in reply, as well as to Lucius himself, certainly appears confirmatory, not only of the whole story, but of a Pope's part in it. But if the date was 167 it was not Eleutherius: if it was 183, it was.

To sum up, it is interesting that English tradition associates Lucius with building churches in four great religious centres, Glastonbury, London, Llandaff,[12] and Gloucester, and that there still stand associated with him St. Michael's on the Tor at Glastonbury, St. Peter's, Cornhill, London, claimed to be the earliest Metropolitan Church of London, and four churches near Llandaff, one actually dedicated to him as Lleurwgg, and the others respectively to Dyfan, Fagan, and Medwy. The Welsh Church commemorated the baptism of King Lucius on May 28, and his Martyrdom on December 3, the latter an interesting commemoration. The Festival of St. Dyfan was kept on April 8, and that of St. Fagan on August 8. They were commemorated together on May 24, obviously part of the King Lucius

[12] Rees's *Welsh Saints* quoting the Welsh Triad 62 of the 3rd Series.

commemoration. St. Elfan's Day was on September 26, and St. Medwy's on January 1.[13]

Geographically and architecturally there is strikingly visible support to these ancient traditions of the early Church at Glastonbury. Just as to the south-west of the little city stands Wyrral Hill, where the feet of the first disciples rested, where once grew the Holy Thorn, so to the south-east looms St. Michael's Tor, visible over half Somerset, and even from other counties, and crowned with the tower of St. Michael's Church, successor of the one wrecked by a severe earthquake in 1275.[14] A lonely church set on a hill far above human habitation bespeaks here, as elsewhere, the site of a primitive Christian church converted from, or taking the place of, a heathen temple. It was the wise custom of our forefathers when a country was won for Christ to consecrate to Him, by crosses or churches, spots which were sacred in the minds of the inhabitants. This explains such lonely churches on hills as St. Michael's. Another is at Churchdown in Gloucestershire, which rises

[13] Rhys Rees's *Welsh Saints.* Pitsaeus (*Relat. Hist. de rebus Anglicis Act.*, 60, 560, n. 50) includes Elvan of Avalon as an illustrious British writer, A.D. 180, and says that he was educated in the School of St. Joseph of Arimathea and wrote *De origine Ecclesiae Britannicae.* Pits or Pitsaeus was an eminent Roman Catholic.

[14] Good King Lucius is said to have built the first St. Michael's in A.D. 167. The date varies a little. Baronius, Vol. 2, gives the year 183 for the Mission from Rome. He contradicts Bede, who says that it happened under Marcus Aurelius and Lucius Verus (the latter died in 169). Baronius insists that Eleutherius was Pope, which fits in with 183. He names Elvan and Medwy Lucius' British messengers to Eleutherius. He mentions that the Christian religion had been brought to Britain long before. He refers to Gildas the Wise's *De Excidio*, which shows that he knew the claim that Christianity came in A.D. 37. And he discusses the fact that part of Britain was under Roman arms, and part not.

sheer out of the plain, the church at the terribly steep top ministering to the hamlets of Hucklecote and Chosen at its base. But the examples are common. It is a relic of Baal or Sun worship, when people worshipped in the groves and high places so often mentioned in the Bible. And it is not at all uncommon to find these loftily-placed, lonely churches dedicated to St. Michael, as here, to signify that Christ and His angels had triumphed over the devil and his angels.

Rather more than one hundred years after the coming of St. Joseph to Glastonbury, and the setting up of his little wattle church, the religion of Christ prevailed. It had been fostered here by King Arviragus, by direct missionary work; by the return of the converted family of King Caractacus straight from the feet of St. Paul; by the coming of Christian Roman soldiers and traders and colonists; by Apostolic and sub-Apostolic missions; and finally consummated by a mission from the Church of the Great Mistress of the World. The temples of Baal fell, and Britain was Christian. The Church of Rome in modern days scoffs at our beautiful British tradition of the Arimathean Mission. She did not do so as long as we were in union with her. And Robert Parsons the great and self-sacrificing Jesuit, a man of noble zeal, embalmed the tradition in his *Three Conversions of England*, viz., by St. Joseph, by SS. Fagan and Dyfan, and by St. Augustine. It is extremely significant that, of the " Three Perpetual Choirs " of Britain, Glastonbury is at the foot of the Tor, once a centre of Druidic worship (as the tower of the Christian church still amidst all weathers and lights triumphantly proclaims north, south, east, and west); and Ambresbury is close to Stonehenge, the great temple of Druidic worship. This dominating Tor rises out of the plain, and is the centre of a great basin ringed round with hills. It is one of the few places in England where you can

see more than a clear mile in every direction, and you can
see many miles in every direction. There is a perpetual
breeze at the top. One wishes that the little church could
be restored, and the hill become a place of pilgrimage for
consumptives, who could breathe the pure air, and rest,
and say their devotions on this age-consecrated spot, and
perchance stop on their downward journey to crave a drink
of water from the medicinal waters of the Chalice Well.[15]
As one stands here on the Tor with an absolutely uninter-
rupted circle of view, one can well understand that the
spot was chosen for the worship of the sun. Perhaps it was
this commanding fane, with the sacred well at its foot,
which led to the presence of the court of Arviragus. Certain
it is there are no lake villages in the Kingdom equal to the
two which lie amid the marshes which surround the town
—those of Godney and Meare—and the remains found in
them date, roughly, from 200 B.C.[16]

[15] After a dream by one Matthew Chancellor in 1750 for a
short time the water was in great demand, and a small spa
was formed. It is a strong chalybeate, reputed to be especially
good for asthma, phthisis and cancer. The spring yields about
25,000 gallons a day, and never lessens. Radio-activity has
been found in it.

[16] Vide " Prehistoric Lake Dwellings," The Times, August
14, 1922, and Dr. Arthur Ballard's The Lake Villages of
Somerset (Folk Press, Ltd.).

CHAPTER 4

TRADITION OF OUR LORD AND THE BLESSED VIRGIN

PERHAPS there is some truth in the strange tradition which still lingers, not only among the hill folk of Somerset, but of Gloucestershire,[1] and in the West of Ireland,[2] that St. Joseph of Arimathea came to Britain first as a metal merchant seeking tin[3] from the Scillies and Cornwall, and lead,[4] copper, and other metals from the hills of Somerset, and that Our Lord Himself came with him as a boy.[5] The

---

[1] The Ven. Walter Farrer, late Archdeacon of Wells, was my authority for this tradition lingering in the hills of Gloucestershire.

[2] The Rev. Canon A. B. R. Young, Prebendary of Clogher, had heard the tradition in Ireland all his life.

[3] A few years back there was dug up at Ostia, the seaport of Rome, an ancient Roman drain-pipe below the chariot road. It was bonded in some special way with tin. Professor Russell Forbes cut off a section, and sent it home to England, without comment, for analysis. The verdict was that the metal came from the Mendip mines.

[4] The two earliest exhibits of Roman-British lead in the British Museum came from the Mendip Hill, near Glaston-bury. One is dated A.D. 49, and has the name of Britannicus, son of the Emperor Claudius, on it. The other, dated A.D. 60, bears the inscription " British lead, the property of the Emperor Nero." It is also said that in the wonderful aqueduct in Jerusalem, attributed to King Solomon, the particular type of lead found in the Mendips and nowhere else was used. This was 1000 B.C.

[5] Mr. E. V. Duff, Count of the Holy Roman Empire, told the author that in Maronite and Catluei villages in Upper Galilee, there lingers a tradition that as a youth Our Lord came to

tradition is so startling that the first impulse is summarily
to reject it as ridiculous. But certain it is that among the
old tin-workers, who have always observed a certain
mystery in their rites, there was a moment when they
ceased their work and started singing a quaint song beginning "Joseph was a tin merchant."[6] And certain it is that
if St. Joseph was a metal merchant he must somehow have
got tin for bronze, and that Britain is almost the sole land
of tin mines; and if he were a metal merchant it is not
inconsistent with his being a rich man. And the strange
story of our Lord's coming, which is so very dear to simple
Somerset hearts, would be explained by the Eastern tradition that St. Joseph was the uncle of the Blessed Virgin
Mary.[7] So if there be any truth in the old story, this
ancient Tor with its rites may have attracted the mart
which first led here St. Joseph and the Redeemer before He
began His ministry. And to it, after the wondrous Resurrection and Ascension, St. Joseph, laden with the New
Message of the New Religion, would wend his way on his
mission from Gaul to Britain, the seat of Druidism. His

Britain as a shipwright aboard a trading vessel of Tyre, and
that He was storm-bound on the shores of the West of
England throughout the winter.

[6] Mr. Henry Jenner, F.S.A., late of the British Museum, son
of the late Bishop Jenner, narrates that some years back in
North London during the making of tin sheets for organ pipes
before the molten tin was poured, a man said every time:
"Joseph was in the tin trade." (*Quarterly Review of the Benedictines of Caldey*, 1916, pp. 135–6, and in a MS. letter to myself
vide appendix 9.)

[7] It is curious that King Arthur claimed descent from St.
Joseph; and St. David, said to be his uncle, was said to be of
kin to the Blessed Virgin Mary. For the descent of King
Arthur see *John of Glastonbury* (Hearne's edition), Vol. 1, pp.
56–57, where it is set out. He was eighth in descent. See also
pp. 12, 37, 38, and W. A. S. Hewin's *The Royal Saints of
Britain*, p. 20, and appendix 3.

knowledge of the Druids would account (in part) for his kindly reception by the Druids of France, and he would come to King Arviragus, or at any rate some of his subjects, as a not unknown person, and hence, perhaps, his kindly reception, and the donation of land.

As the years go on, and wider knowledge comes, this wonderful story of Our Lord's own visit to Somerset and Cornwall, immortalized by William Blake in his

" And did those feet in ancient days
        Walk upon England's mountains green? "

grows more and more upon one. The possibilities are great. Between the ages of 12 and 30 we know nothing of Our Lord's life. He might well have accompanied his uncle St. Joseph on a voyage. My mere collecting of the traditions in one little book has fired so many, that they are searching and collecting traditions from Cornwall as well as Somerset. The well-known Cornish ones, such as the Marazion one, always referred to Our Lord coming as a child with the Blessed Virgin Mary; the Somerset ones, to his coming as a lad with St. Joseph of Arimathea. Both may be true; I shall show that there appears to have been some connection by marriage or blood between the Blessed Virgin Mary and the British Royal Family. The Rev. C. C. Dobson, Vicar of St. Mary in the Castle, Hastings, one of those fired, presses the matter further and suggests that Our Lord actually stayed some time in Glastonbury and built a wattle building.[8] He bases this mainly on the letter, quoted by myself in this and former editions of this book, from St. Augustine to Pope Gregory the Great, where he records the claim that the first followers of Christ visiting Britain "God beforehand acquainting them, found a Church constructed by no human art, but by the Hands of Christ

[8] *Did Our Lord Visit Britain?* by Rev. C. C. Dobson.

Himself for the salvation of His people." One's natural impulse is to regard this statement as simply absurd exaggeration, the more so as it is claimed that the building was constructed by no human art. And as such I have always regarded it. But in view of Mr. Dobson's suggestion, one must remember that, under such an exaggeration as that no human art built the building, there might lurk a lingering tradition that Our Lord had built, or taken part in constructing, a building in Britain during a visit as a youth, which tallies with Our Lord being brought up in the home of a carpenter. Mr. Dobson thinks that the very strange name for Glastonbury "the Secret of the Lord" supports this theory. It would at least be a possible explanation. "Secretum" can certainly mean a place of retirement. Mr. Dobson further has got hold of a tradition which had not reached me, that Christ and St. Joseph came in a ship of Tarshish to the summer-land, and sojourned in a place called Paradise.[9] Of course Somerset is often called the Summerland. Mr. Dobson has discovered that at a seaside place called Burnham, seventeen miles from Glastonbury, there is a farm called Paradise Farm[10] in a district round Burnham called Paradise in the old ordnance surveys maps, and he links that name with Our Lord's traditional visit. He does not appear to know that a part of Glastonbury itself is called Paradise, and that a beautiful little spot north-east of Glastonbury Tor also bears the same name,[11] and an ancient road leading from it is still called Paradise Lane. It is a curious name, but the name of the latter spot is probably a lingering memory of Celtic

[9] Since corroborated to me by Mr. E. V. Duff, who has spent ten years in Palestine and speaks Aramaic, the language which Our Lord spoke (*vide* p. 64).

[10] *Did Our Lord visit Britain?*, p. 24.

[11] *Vide* the Author's *Glastonbury, the Mother of Saints*, p. 35, 2nd edition.

days, when Avalon was Avilion, and the spirits of the
departed were supposed to pass through the Tor. And a
piece of land to the south-west of the Tor bears the name
Avalon in an old Church Terrier. But this explanation
makes it all the more strange that a piece of Glastonbury
itself, geographically remote from the dell near the Tor,
bears the name Paradise. So, as the possibility of a sojourn
of some length has been raised, one might refer to another
strange name recorded by Sir Robert Wingfield, Henry
VIII's Ambassador to the Emperor Maximilian. After the
claims of precedence of British Bishops at the early 15th-
century Church Councils on the ground of the Glastonbury
Arimathean story, Sir Robert Wingfield had the Acts of
the Council of Constance recorded. Archbishop Ussher
wrote (Cap. 2) of the two existing MSS. of this: one in
the Royal Library; another, formerly the property of
Cardinal Peter Bembi, but then in the library of Sir Henry
Wootton.

Now how deeply rooted in the English mind was the
importance of the Arimathean Tradition, is not only
shown by the fact, as Professor Skeat has shown,[12] that
directly printing began, Wynkyn de Worde printed one,
and Pynson two, ancient accounts of it. But Mr. E. M.
Tenison has drawn my attention to the fact that not only
did Sir Robert Wingfield, Henry VIII's Ambassador, have
the proceedings of the Council of Constance recorded one
hundred years after its sitting, but Queen Elizabeth
claimed precedence, citing her father's claim, and based it
on this very ground: "Joseph of Arimathea planted
Christian Religion immediately after the Passion of Christ
in this Realme." This claim was solemnly made "at Calais
before Commissioners appointed by the French King".
Sir Henry Nevill "had moved a Treaty of Peace in this

[12] Skeat's *Joseph of Arimathie*, Oxford University Press, 1871
and 1924.

unfortunate yeare of the reign of the same Queene by Robert Cotton Esquire at the commandment of the Queen's Majesty ".[13] More startling still is the fact that this information of Queen Elizabeth's action is recorded in an eight-page quarto pamphlet " printed in London by L. N. and N. C. for Thomas Slater at the Signe of the Swan in Duck Lane, November, 1642 "—in the time of Charles I, when nothing might be printed without a licence. Thus, from Henry IV's reign (1409) to Charles I's (1642)—233 years—the Glastonbury Tradition was the basis of great national claims. It was used just as William I's historical refusal to do homage to the Pope was used. It is reserved for modern critics to embalm themselves by an easy scepticism. As Dryden wrote about the critics of his time:

> Pretty in amber to see dirt and flies and straw.
> The things themselves are neither rich nor rare.
> One wonders how the devil they got there.

In Sir Robert Wingfield's record appears the very strange expression, "Immediately after the passion of Christ, Joseph of Arimathea the noble Decurio[14] . . . immediately

[13] The author has a little book published in 1651 by Francis Leach for Henry Stile by St. Dunstan's Church, Fleet Street, called *Cotton's Posthuma*, being choice pieces of the celebrated Sir Robert Cotton. No. 4 contains an account of the English claim to precedency at Church Councils " collected by Robert Cotton (then) Esquire at the commandments of Her Majesty ".

[14] We have proof that Decurio was a recognized office in the Roman Empire in the time of St. Joseph. Cicero had a favourite villa in Pompeii. At that time its City Council consisted of Decurios, who had been ex-magistrates, and of other pre-eminent persons. So important were they, that Cicero said with some irony that it was easier to become a Senator of Rome than a Decurio in Pompeii. Did King Arviragus give St. Joseph authority as a Decurio in the mining district of the Mendips? British Princes had been brought up at the Court of Augustus.

proceeded to cultivate THE LORD'S VINEYARD, THAT IS TO SAY
ENGLAND, and converted the peoples to the Faith." It goes
on to speak of the grant of the Twelve Hides of Glaston,
and his burial in that place. Why should England be
called the Lord's Vineyard? It is a curious name for it.
One feels bound to record that on the south side of Weary
All Hill, which is the traditional landing or resting place
of St. Joseph and his eleven companions, is a piece of land
still called the Vineyard. Right down to the time of the
Dissolution the monks actually cultivated it as a vineyard.
While this would be quite sufficient to explain the name,
it does not wipe out the possibility of the place being kept
as a vineyard because of very ancient and sacred memories.
If Our Lord had any connection with a vineyard there,
the unbroken spiritual descendants of the first anchorites
would have been likely to have kept it on as such. It is
amazing how mere custom will become the handmaid of
a tradition. I will cite a Glastonbury instance. When I
went to Glastonbury as Vicar there were on the west end
of the north wall of the nave of the church, in a large
case, two ancient pieces of needlework, one plainly a pall,
the other a mysterious square which when unfolded some
years later turned out to be an oblong. There was a tradition about the pall; none about the other. The tradition
was that the pall had been made out of a cope which had
once been worn by Abbot Whiting, the last and martyred
Abbot, in the Parish Church. (After 1220 the Abbots were
Rectors of the church.) I sent, my first summer, to Cardiff
Museum for an expert opinion, and told them the tradition.
It came, and the verdict was, "Both pieces of the same
period and exactly of that period." The history of the
pieces was that until they were lent to the Glastonbury
Museum, when the case was made, they had always been
kept in a very old chest in the old school. Some years later,
when the case was moved to the North Transept I had keys

made for it. It was then found that the folded square was an oblong.

Shortly after, I was taking a Roman Catholic monk, a priest from Woolhampton, round the church. He was greatly excited at the smaller piece, and explained that it was a Gremial, or apron only worn by Bishops, with the single exception of Benedictine Abbots (and no others), if sitting down when pontificating, so that their hot hands should not spoil their rich vestments. It was a whole garment which had belonged to Abbot Whiting. The tradition has been lost. But because worn by him the two garments had been placed in the same chest. The cope had been converted into a pall, and the tradition of its revered wearer remained. Still the lesser garment was kept with the pall in the same old chest by custom. When the pall was removed into the case, by custom the apron went with it, folded up to fit in. And at length when, many years after, it was unfolded, its history was unfolded too. Preserved blindly by custom in the same case with its companion, the fact that only a Benedictine Abbot or a Bishop could have worn it, coupled with its being of exactly the same period as Abbot Whiting's cope (changed into a pall) revealed who the wearer must have been. Thus will custom and tradition go hand in hand. The facts that England was specifically called " The Lord's Vineyard " in connection with Joseph of Arimathea at the Council of Constance, and that, on the hill where he traditionally landed, is a spot called the Vineyard, and that there are these traditions about Our Lord having visited Glastonbury, must not be pressed too far. But in view of Mr. Dobson's suggestion I record the facts.

Before I leave this subject I would mention something which has always puzzled me. On the south side of St. Mary's Chapel, the Norman successor of the old wattle church, without any apparent rhyme or reason there

appears in the wall a little old stone with two names " Jesus
Maria " in large archaic letters.

Archbishop Ussher[15] tells us William Goode's, the
Jesuit's, recollections of Glastonbury Abbey. He was a
server in St. Mary's when eight years old, and twelve years
old when the Abbey fell. It is strange that among the few
things that he recollects as an old man abroad he empha-
sizes this stone. These are his words: " Moreover, outside,
in the wall of this Chapel of the Blessed Virgin, there were
carved in stone in characters of great age these two words
' Jesus Maria.' " Why suddenly in that wall do those two
names appear? The monks evidently attached a great
veneration to that stone. Did the feet of these holy beings
named ever tread this spot? I instinctively take off my hat
when I approach it. It is a hallowed spot. Is Mr. Dobson
right in pressing St. Augustine's words? No one will ever
know. But it is a hallowed spot. The very possibility
sanctifies beyond all words. One hopes it is true. And those
who seek may find. It makes Our Lord seem very near.

While our minds still linger on the mysterious traditions
linking the names of the Blessed Virgin and Our Lord
with these shores, may one not be permitted to wonder
whether some of them at least do not suggest a further
reason than previous acquaintance for the kindly reception
by King Arviragus of St. Joseph. Is it possible that
Arviragus was related to St. Joseph and the Blessed Virgin
Mary? In the Grail stories Avallach or Evalake is frequently mentioned, and how St. Joseph converted and
baptized him. It must be remembered that these stories of
the Grail and of the Knights of the Round Table hail from
Glastonbury. They are nothing less than Glastonbury's
two great stories of St. Joseph and King Arthur strangely
and inextricably interwoven. The successive devastating

[15] *Brit. Eccl. Antiquitates*, Cap. 2 (H. Kendra Baker's translation), pp. 43–45.

invasions of the heathen Saxons and Danes, followed by
the Norman one with its Roman, if less devastating influence, had almost wiped out the memory of the glorious
missionary Apostolic British Church save in a few places.
It was re-awakened by the discovery of Arthur's body in
A.D. 1190–1191. We have the account of two eye-witnesses
of the disinterment. With the discovery of Arthur's body[16]
the two great Glastonbury stories re-awoke. It was the
halcyon age of the troubadours. They carried the two
stories interwoven like warp and woof through Europe in
the Lays of the Round Table.[17]

Rolleston in his *Myths and Legends of the British Race*
has some most informing remarks about the origin of the
Lays of the Round Table. He traces their origin to Britain
and Brittany.

It is well known that Geoffrey of Monmouth claimed
that his *History of the British* was the translation of an
ancient British book given to him by Walter, Archdeacon
of Oxford. Geoffrey of Monmouth was Bishop of St.
Asaph, and Walter Mapes, Archdeacon of Oxford, was his
uncle. It is equally well known that Walter Mapes
embalmed the Round Table stories. It is fashionable to
discredit Geoffrey of Monmouth's history as all myths and
fiction, and a forgery. No book more glorifies the ancient
British race. Without claiming that the book is all gospel
truth, it is reasonable to ask its disparagers—what motive
had Geoffrey of Monmouth in forging such a history?
Geoffrey was half a Norman, half a Saxon. Why should
he forge a history glorifying the British race? One prefers
his statement that it was a translation of an old British

---

[16] *Vide* author's *Glastonbury, the Mother of Saints*, pp.
34–37.
[17] See author's *Glastonbury, Mother of Saints*, p. 41.

book which fell into Archdeacon Mape's hands, and that
he handed it to his Episcopal nephew who translated it.

Rolleston tells that Wace translated Geoffrey of Monmouth's book into French under the title of *Li Romans
de Brut* about 1155,—Geoffrey traces the coming of Brutus,
first King of Britain (great-grandson of Aesneas of Troy)
about 1130 B.C.—and that Layamon translated *Li Romans*
into Anglo-Saxon, and so anticipated Malory's adaptation
of later French prose romances (p. 338). He also says that
Walter the Archdeacon claimed that he got his book from
Brittany (p. 337). He further tells that about 1150 Marie
de France, who repeatedly claimed Breton sources, wrote
a number of Lais in French placing them " in Arthur's
time ", mentioning the Round Table and the Isle d' Avalon
and showing that there was in Brittany a thorough knowledge of the Arthurian stories (pp. 339–40). Rolleston
further tells that it was not till about 1165 that Chretien de
Troyes began also to translate Breton Lais, and that he, not
Walter Mapes, introduced the Lancelot story, but Marie de
France had told of one Lenval who had loved Guinevere,
but rejected her because he had a fairy mistress in the Isle
d' Avalon (pp. 339–340).

Gautier de Denain, the first to write after Chretien, gives
as his authority for the Gawain stories, Bleheris, a poet
" born and bred in Wales ", while Giraldus Cambrennis
gives a Bledherius (doubtless the same name, badly
Latinized) and Thomas of Brittany Breris (probably the
same name again confused) as an authority for the Tristan
story (p. 341). Dr. Heinrich Zimmer claims that in Welsh
literature there is definite evidence that the South Wales
Prince Rhys ap Tewdur brought from Brittany in 1070 the
knowledge of Arthur's Round Table (p. 343).

Incidentally we may mention that Rolleston says that
Avalon implies a " Land of the Dead ". This is interesting
as the name " Avilion " once applied to Avalon means

"Departed Spirits", and there is the local claim that departed spirits passed through the Tor.

One is glad to see that he too does not reject Geoffrey of Monmouth's wonderful history, tracing the British race back to Troy. He points out that Nennius in his *Historia Britonum,* about A.D. 800, also tells the Trojan story, and he stresses that there is a Troyes in Champagne in France, where Chretien de Troyes was born. It should be recorded that both Lord Chief Justice Coke and Lord Chancellor Fortescue stated that the foundation of the British Common Law was Trojan.

We have emphasized the constant early intercourse between Britain and Brittany and it must be remembered that later, in the 10th century, the Plantagenet Counts of Blois, and the Dukes of Brittany, intermarried. There can be little doubt that the Arthurian Lays started in England, and that Glastonbury was their centre.

The kindliness of Arviragus to St. Joseph makes it of great interest that the Bardic pedigrees of Welsh princes and saints are constantly traced to this Aballach, Avalloch or Evelake. Welsh pedigrees scorn dates and have many discrepancies, but beneath them lies some sub-stratum of fact. No less than four of these British royal pedigrees trace up to a Beli and an Anna, cousin or consobrina of the Blessed Virgin Mary; and one of them (St. David's, reported uncle of King Arthur) traces to Euguen, son of the sister of the Blessed Virgin Mary.[18] Each of these pedigrees has Avallach in them. So here is a distinct claim to some kinship between the British Royal Family and the Blessed Virgin Mary, and so with St. Joseph of Arimathea,

[18] See p. 12 and also W. A. S. Hewin's *Royal Saints of Britain,* p. 20. For Avallach see also Dr. Davey Bigg's *Ictis and Avallon,* pp. 28, 31.

reputed by Eastern tradition to have been her uncle. This
might account for Arviragus's kindness to St. Joseph (see
Appendix 3).

Here it is that a wonderful Breton tradition, which I owe
to Sir Courtenay Bennett, comes in. Details differ, but how
can one expect perfect accuracy in these most ancient tales?
The noticeable thing is how much they tally and interlock.
This tradition again links the Holy Family by marriage
with Britain, this time with Cornwall, where there linger
memories of Our Lord as a babe, and the Blessed Virgin
Mary having visited Marazion. Priddy, among the mines
of the Mendips, shares with its neighbouring Glastonbury
the tradition of Our Lord having visited there with St.
Joseph of Arimathea when a lad (see Appendix 6). The
Breton story runs thus (again an Anna is involved, but this
time it is definitely St. Anna, mother of the Blessed Virgin,
and she is linked with Cornwall): Anna was born in
Cornouaille, of royal blood. Brutally treated by a jealous
husband, when with child, she fled toward the sea; an
angel caused her to enter a vessel, and took her to Asia to
Jaffa, where she landed, and whence she reached Nazareth.
There she gave birth to a little girl, whom she named
Mary. When the child was fifteen years old, she was
married to a carpenter, named Joseph, and Anna then
prayed to God to take her back to Cornouaille. The same
angel again took her over the waves. Anna found that her
husband was dead, divided her property among his vassals,
and ended her days beside the bay of Palue near the well,
which is still to be seen there, in a little cot, where Jesus
came several times to visit her. When she died her body
vanished. This tradition is told in Hachette's *Guide Bleu,
Bretagne*. St. Anna de la Palue is one of the chief patron
saints in Brittany. I learn with immense interest from the
Rev. H. A. Lewis, late Vicar of Talland in Cornwall, in
whose parish lay the ancient Isle and former Priory of

Lammana, once belonging to Glastonbury Abbey, that Lammana was of old divided into Parlooe and Portlooe, that there was a St. Anna's Well there, that a chapel on old Looe Bridge was dedicated to St. Anna, as was also a church at Hessenford,[19] five miles distant. Could Lammana be Lan Anna, the Church of Anna? Lammana was actually called Sancta Lamana (Holy Lamana) in the Taxation of Pope Nicholas IV, A.D. 1288–91. This is happily preserved in the Diocesan Registry, Exeter. It is the version of David Anselm, Rector of Tedburn St. Mary, and is appended to the MS. Register of Bishop Bromscombe in the Exeter Diocesan Registry. Prebendary Hingeston-Randolph edited it, and believed it to be, if not contemporary, nearly so, and " very full and accurate, much more so than any other copies referred to above ". Anselm resigned the living of Tedburn in 1332.[20]

Glastonbury, which shared similar stories of the coming of members of the Holy Family, treasured Lammana Priory as she did Basselake Priory in Wales, which had dim traditions about St. Joseph and a Holy Thorn, and

[19] What relation has this name to Essa's Bed, a rock just off Llammana? Can these words be a corruption of Jesu or of the Hebrew for Joseph, Jusef? For further enquiry into these most interesting traditions, see the Rev. H. A. Lewis's *The Child Christ at Lammana*, and *Ab Antiquo*. Mr. E. V. Duff, before mentioned (*vide* p. 54), who speaks fluently several Eastern languages, tells that Isa, pronounced Eesa, is the Aramaic (the language which Our Lord spoke) for Jesus. He spent ten years in Palestine.

[20] Sir Courtenay Bennett, the Rev. C. C. Dobson, and the Rev. H. A. Lewis, have all been fired by the mere simple statement of Glastonbury's wonderful story and that of the Celtic Church in these isles in former editions of this little book. Their enthusiasm and that of many others has been most helpful, and partly accounts for the increase of the first edition's sixteen pages of actual matter and four illustrations to the size of this edition.

had stronger traditions about King Arthur. The French think that the hut in the above tradition was in the Bay of La Palue in Brittany. But when one remembers that Brittany was peopled with the victorious Britons who over-ran the continent in 387 under the Emperor Maximus Magnus[21] and that after the defeat of Aurelius Ambrosius (probably the uncle of King Arthur) much of the remaining flower of British manhood fled to Brittany, including the bishops, clergy, and laity, with their traditions; that they were constantly replenished by harried Christians during later heathen Saxon raids; it is much more natural to suppose that the Cornish ones took with them their cherished Cornish traditions, cults, and place-names, than that an isolated French one somehow got engrafted into Cornwall. The likelihood is increased by the fact that, at the immigration of Britons under King Rivallous, or Howell, with a multitude of ships in 512, Bishoprics were founded for them by Childebert at Leon and perhaps at Dol. The Archbishopric of Tours was already a British foundation.[22] Thus in the land of their kindred, ruled over by kings of the same royal stock, St. Anna became the patron saint of Brittany. All these West of England stories have the same sheen. Traditions? Oh, yes. Inexact? Oh, yes. But through them all runs the same thought like a thread of gold. And would any one have dared to invent completely the story of St. Anna at Parlooe?

I have also been informed that at the Ding Dong Mine at Penwith (roughly the Land's End district from St. Ives

[21] Sozomen, *Hist. Eccl.*, VII, 13. Haddan and Stubbs, Vol. 1, p. 12. W. A. S. Hewin's *Royal Saints of Britain*, pp. 39–43. The Emperor Maximus Magnus or Maxen Wledi was a Romano-Spaniard related to the Emperor Theodosius, and of the family of Constantine the Great, and of British Royal descent on his mother's side. Several great Welsh families claim descent from him. (See also p. 109.)

[22] Haddan and Stubbs, Vol. 2, and see later p. 109.

to Penzance) the following story is told : that St. Joseph, the
foster-father of Our Lord, used to come as a ship's carpenter
there frequently to get tin, and that on one occasion he
brought Our Lord. A former curate at Newlyn, I understand, came across frequent references to the same story
when visiting his parishioners, within the last twenty
years. This is, of course, a variant of the story of Our
Lord coming once with St. Joseph of Arimathea—possibly
a confusion very likely to arise in the course of ages.
I have already mentioned in a footnote at the beginning
of " The Tradition of Our Lord, and the Blessed Virgin "
that Mr. E. V. Duff told me that he found a tradition in
Maronite and Catluci villages in Northern Galilee that Our
Lord came to Britain as a shipwright in a trading vessel
from Tyre, and wintered once in Britain. The two traditions from widely distant lands have resemblances, and
add to the varied and cumulative evidence that the Holy
Family had some connection with this land.

The Rev. H. A. Lewis has drawn my attention to a word
in the celebrated passage in Melchinus (or Maelgwyn)
" who was before Merlin ", beginning " Insula Avallonis
avida funera paganorum."[23] This is the passage which tells
of St. Joseph's burial in Avalon, with the two cruets.
Everyone's attention has been focused on the point in it,
which Dean Armitage Robinson called " an age-long
puzzle ", as to the exact spot where St. Joseph was buried
and whether " in lineâ bifurcatâ " points to a locality or
a garment. Few have given the meticulously careful and
loving scholarly attention which Mr. Lewis has given to
details in the Arimathean Tradition. And we all have most
shamefully neglected to notice one most startling word.
It is the word *super* in the passage " Et jacet in lineâ

[23] Hearne's *John of Glastonbury*, small edition, p. 30; also
MS. Cotton *Titus*, D. VII, fol. 29-b; and MS. Arundel, 230, fol.
274, John of Tinmuth.

bifurcatâ juxta meridianum angulum oratorii, cratibus preparatis, *super* potentem adorandam Virginem supradictis spherulatis locum habitantibus tredecim." The word *super* can only mean "over" or "above". The passage means " He [St. Joseph] lies in a bifurcated line [or bifurcated linen garment] next the southern corner of the oratory made of wattles *over* the powerful adorable Virgin." The simple plain meaning is that she lies buried there. This is indeed startling. It recalls to us all the amazing statements about this spot: that the archangel St. Gabriel ordered its erection in honour of St. Mary[24]; that Our Lord Himself dedicated it in honour of His Mother[25]; that it is called " the Holiest Earth in England "[26]; that it was built by the hands of Christ's Disciples[27]; that St. Joseph has the same word applied to him as to St. John the Evangelist, " paranymphos "[28] or attendant to the Blessed Virgin; that he is stated to have been present at her assumption[29]; that frequently his coming to Britain is dated from her assumption[30]; that the two words " Jesu Maria " mysteriously appear on the south wall of this chapel and that William Goode, the old monk in exile, remembered this as one of the things most to be recollected of this place; that William of Malmesbury in his *Acts of the Kings of the English* (earlier than his *De Antiquitate Glastoniæ*) wrote (Bk. 1,

[24] MS. Cotton *Titus*, D. VII, and MS. Arundel, 220. Malmesbury, Cap. 1.

[25] MS. Cotton *Titus*, D. VII. MS. Arundel, 220. Hearne's *John of Glastonbury*, p. 2. MS. of Malmesbury, Cap. 1.

[26] Pynson's *Life of Joseph of Arimathia*, line 369.

[27] Malmesbury, Cap. 1.

[28] *Magna Tabula Glastoniæ* at Naworth. *Vide* also p. 94.

[29] *De Sancto Joseph ab Arimathia*, by Richard Pynson. *Magna Tabula Glastoniæ*, etc.

[30] William of Malmesbury's *Glastonbury*, Cap. 1 and *Magna Tabula Glastoniæ*.

cap. 2) thus: "The church of which we are speaking—from its antiquity called by the Angles, by way of distinction 'Ealde Chiche', that is the 'Old Church' of wattle work at first, savoured somewhat of heavenly sanctity even from its very foundation, and exhaled it over the whole country, claiming superior reverence, though the structure was mean[31] . . . at night scarcely any one presumes to keep vigil there, or during the day to spit upon the floor: he who is conscious of pollution shudders throughout his whole frame. No one ever brought hawk or horses within the confines of the neighbouring cemetery who did not depart injured, either in them, or himself . . . the men of that province had no oath more frequent, or more sacred than to swear by the Old Church, fearing the swiftest vengeance on their perjury in this respect. . . . In the meantime it is clear that the depository of so many saints may be deservedly called an heavenly sanctuary upon earth . . . who there more especially chose to await the day of resurrection under the protection of the mother of God."

These words show the sanctity of St. Mary's Church, Glastonbury. The plain meaning of the passage in Melchinus is that the Blessed Virgin was buried there. Only a limited portion of the public believe in her assumption, perhaps the greatest assumption that ever was conceived. When Palestine was no longer safe for her, did St. Joseph, her relative and paranymphos, by delegated authority bring her to the peace of Avalon to end her days in the Britain which tradition claims she had known in earlier days, and with which she was linked through her mother by race, possibly to the spot where she had been with Our Lord? Did St. Joseph watch her die there, and did he bury her there? The earliest written record claims

---

[31] He expressly adds a suggestion that "the stones of the pavement designedly interlaid in triangles and squares, and figured with lead, contain some sacred enigma".

her burial there. The church was always dedicated to her.
This has always been a stumbling block to those learned
in church dedications. It was not till the 12th century that
dedications to St. Mary began. The earliest dedications
were either to the Blessed Trinity, St. Michael, or the
memory of a local saint who was buried there, the latter
by far the most common. Was St. Mary buried there?
Any local tradition lingering through the ravages of the
Saxons and Danes would unfortunately be swamped by the
Norman influence with its Roman traditions. The Eastern
Church keeps the festival of the Assumption as the
Koimesis, the falling asleep. The Gnostics in the 4th
century started a legend that St. Mary lived at Bethlehem
after her son's death, till an angel came to say that she
must die; that she was borne in a cloud to Jerusalem, and
carried by the Apostles to Gethsemane, where her soul was
received by St. Gabriel and carried to Paradise; that the
Apostles bore her body to the valley of JEHOSAPHAT, and
laid it in a new tomb; that Our Lord appeared, ordered St.
Michael to bring her soul from Paradise, re-united it to her
body, and entrusted her to angels to carry her to heaven.
Epiphanius (Haer 89) denounced this story thus: " The
whole thing is foolish and strange, and is a device and
deceit of the devil." The saintly Pope Gelasius condemned
the book (*De Transitu Virginis Mariae Liber*) as heretical
in the year 494. Nevertheless the Festival of the Assumption was instituted by the Emperor Maurice at the beginning of the 7th century. Charlemagne rejected it. His son
Lewis accepted it in 818. Today under August 15 it is
found in the Roman Breviary. There too we read that the
Apostles carried the body to the valley of JEHOSAPHAT.[32]
It is not without interest to those who explore traditions
that the passage in Melkinus, from which quotation has

[32] It must be realized that this refers to her dead body.

already been made, says that in the Isle of Avalon "sleeps
Abbadare, powerful in SHAPHAT, noblest of pagans [country
folk] along with 104,000 " and that the passage ends thus:
" For a long time before the Day of Judgment shall these
things [the discovery of St. Joseph's body] be open and
declared to living men in JEHOSAPHAT."[33]

Here, then, is a new problem, which will never be solved.
Was St. Mary buried in Avalon? We must never forget
that the old Celtic traditions were buried beneath the ruins
of Saxon and Danish invasions, and devastations, and any
that remained were transformed by Norman influence, and
its close association with the great Western Church of
Rome. As we have seen, it was not till the exhumation of
Arthur's body in the 12th century that the two great
Glastonbury stories of St. Joseph and Arthur were revived,
and circulated in a jumbled form—the Grail stories (see
Appendix 4). It was in that very century that the cult of
St. Mary was developed, and that church dedications to
her were superimposed on hosts of earlier local saints'
dedications. But if the wattle church was built over her, it
would have been called after her from the first. The fact
that the moment printing began Wynkyn de Worde
printed a life of St. Joseph, and Pynson two lives, shows
the importance that was attached to the Arimathean
tradition. Pynson in his metrical life of St. Joseph of
Arimathea has the following passage.

Now hear how Joseph came into Englande;
But at that tyme it was called Brytayne.
Than XV yere with our lady, as I understande.
Joseph wayted styll to serve hyr he was fayne.

[33] It must not be forgotten that Avalon was earlier Avilion,
the Isle of Departed Spirits, and so might well be called the
British Vale of Jehosaphat. To the Jews the Valley of
Jehosaphat was the valley of final judgment. Joel iii, 2, 12,
and Dr. William Smith's *Dictionary of the Bible*, I, 95.

So AFTER HYR ASSUMPCYON, the boke telleth playne;
With Saynt Phylyp he went into France.[34]
Phylyp bad them go to Great Brytayn fortunate.[35]

These words might imply, as generally stated, that St. Joseph came to Britain fifteen years after the Assumption; but they might be taken to imply that he was with the Blessed Virgin fifteen years, and then went to France and thence again to Britain. If she died and was buried at Glastonbury, was he with her fifteen years or part of that time there? Gildas called him a noble " decurion ". And in the Latin versions of the Gospels he is called the same. Dr. Davey Biggs says that this " was the regular term in the Roman Empire for the officers placed in charge of the metal mines ".[36] Was he in charge of the Mendip district? His strangely favourable reception as a missionary suggests his being extremely well known previously. One more question I must raise. Why is England known as ' 'Our Lady's Dowry "? Even in far Italy, in Assisi, England is so referred to.[37] True, Richard II is said to have given England as the dowry of the Blessed Virgin. But how or why? More likely he stressed a well-known title. Did the Charter of Henry III (in which he called this church " The Mother of Saints " and the " Tomb of Saints " " built by the Disciples of the Lord and first dedicated by

[34] Lines 113-118. It should be noted that in line 115 the writer refers to tradition for the fifteen years spent with the Blessed Virgin, and in line 117 to a history for his departure to France and Britain after the Assumption. The *Magna Tabula Glastoniæ* at Naworth, as cited by Ussher (Cap. 2), gives the order of events thus: (1) attachment of St. Joseph and his son to St. Philip, and baptism by him; (2) "afterwards" St. Joseph's appointment as Paranymphos by St. John; (3) presence with *St. Philip* and other disciples at the Assumption; (4) fifteen years later, mission to Britain.

[35] Line 124. " Fortunate " from what association?

[36] *Ictis and Avallon*, pp. 32 and 41.

[37] See E. Hutton's *Highways and Byways in Wiltshire*, p. 84.

the Lord Himself ") for which statements he claimed
"venerable authority of the ancients" refer to a literal
personal choice of that place, when it said that "the most
Blessed Virgin chose it for herself specially and first in the
Kingdom ". In view of other statements, who can say?

I learnt from the Rev. H. A. Lewis a distinctly startling
statement. Mrs. Cottrell, of Penwerris, Cornwall, an old
lady, educated as a girl at a French convent in Alexandria
by nuns who were members of the old French *noblesse*,
said that she had been told by the sisters that St. Joseph
of Arimathea brought the Blessed Virgin to Britain, and
that she died there. It is an amazing statement to come
from modern Roman Catholics. At the most it could only
mean that among the French there lingered a tradition
that the Blessed Virgin had come to Britain, and that her
Koimesis, or falling asleep, took place there. After all,
death is a falling asleep.

CHAPTER 5

TOPICAL SUPPORT OF THE TRADITIONS

But let us return to the geography and place names of Glastonbury. Glastonbury Tor is one of the glories of the West Country. As it rises mystic, majestic, romantic, and sacred from the Vale of Avalon, the eyes of all homing travellers and all pilgrims seek it, and rejoice. Whether seen from the top of the Mendips over Wells, or from the Polden Hills above Street and Butleigh, or drawing one on with its beautiful conical shape on the journey from Shepton Mallet, or on the nearer journey from Street to Glastonbury where one sees clearly the thousands-of-years-old path ascending it, it leaves a haunting image on the brain. An Eastern traveller, Dr. Dakhyl, assured the writer that the Tor is very reminiscent of Mount Tabor, which the Arabs of today call Jabal al Torre, which means the Hill of the Tor. One wonders whether the sight of the Tor endeared Glastonbury to St. Joseph, possibly before he came there as a missionary, linking the place to the memory of his homeland.

When considering the subject of the St. Joseph traditions it is worth enlarging on the fact that St. Joseph is called "nobilis decurio" by Gildas Badonicus.[1] Dr. C. R. Davey Biggs, in his little book *Ictis and Avallon*, says that in Spain "a decurio was established in every little mining centre, being charged with the care of the farms, the water supply, the sanitary arrangements, and the local fortifications"

[1] In his *Acts of the Illustrious King Arthur*, John of Glastonbury, small edition, p. 55. Joseph is so described also in some ancient verses, John of Glastonbury, p. 56.

73

It is interesting to find that the term "decurio" is connected with mining districts. St. Joseph became head of
the grant of lands by Arviragus. Dr. Biggs very strongly
claims that Avalon or Glastonbury, with its Tor dedicated
to St. Michael, and not St. Michael's Mount in Cornwall,
was Ictis or Mictis. He bases his argument mainly on
Pliny's quotation (IV, 30) of Timaeus, "Six days sail
inland from Britain there is an island called Mictis in
which white lead is found, and to this island the Britons
come in boats of osier covered with sewn hides"; and on
Diodorus Siculus's[2] (V. 21, 22–31) quotation of Posidonius
who travelled in Britain about 80 B.C. and describes the
metal workers of Balerion or Cornwall carrying their tin
"to a certain island lying off the coast of Britain, called
Ictis; for as the ground between is *left dry at low tide* they
carry tin there in great abundance in their waggons."[3] He
goes on to say of neighbouring islands, "at the high tides
the intervening ground is flooded, and they seem like
islands, but at the low tides, when the sea recedes, and
leaves much space dry, they seem peninsulas. At this
island [Ictis] the merchants buy the tin from the natives
of Britain and carry it across into Gaul." Dr. Biggs argues
that St. Michael's Mount is not six days sail from Cornwall,
that St. Michael's Mount at that date was not cut off by
the sea at high tide, that St. Michael's Mount has no
adjacent islands, but that Glastonbury Manor had in its
domain ten such exactly answering to the above description. There is to this day to the south-west of the Tor a

---

[2] Diodorus Siculus traces, in the last century B.C., the route
of tin merchants from Marseilles to Cornwall. There is an
ancient roadway from the tin mines of Cornwall to the
Somerset lead mines in the Mendips. Some traces still exist.

[3] This would have to be from the mainland, by the causeway
between Glastonbury and Street, where Pompartes Bridge now
is.

farm with the peculiar name of Actis, on which stands the great Abbey Barn. Dr. Biggs also points out that "We have at Glastonbury a centre or junction for roads leading up from Cornwall, and stretching north and west to Rollsright, and Arborlow, to Kit's Coty House, and Coldrum", and cites R. Hippisley Cox's *Green Roads of England*. I may point out that at Rollright in Oxfordshire there is a Druidical circle, another at Arborlow, which is in Derbyshire, and that Kit's Coty House in Kent is a most celebrated cromlech, and that other ancient stones are there. If Dr. Biggs be right in his contention that Glastonbury is Ictis, the island where metal was brought for foreign export, it certainly gives support to the story that St. Joseph came to Glastonbury as a metal merchant before he came there as a missionary, and would account for friendly reception by King Arviragus and the Druids, and for his choice of the spot for his mission.

On the Glastonbury Tor the processional ways of the Druids seem clearly visible.[4] And the marvellous two-chambered Druidical well (said to be so like an Egyptian one) known as the Chalice Well,[5] still pours out at the foot of the Tor its ceaseless flood, which through the generosity of its owner alone, saved the little city from drought in 1921 and again in 1922. It stands in the grounds of what was formerly a hostel, known as Chalice Well Hostel, belonging to the late Miss A. M. Buckton, the gifted authoress of *Eager Heart*, who had so caught the spirit of

[4] Some think them fortifications, and the name of Bulwark Lane at the foot of the Tor lends colour to this, and some most ancient cultivation rings for primitive dwellers above the floods, and their foes. All theories may be right. At Ponter's Ball on the eastern boundary of the parish there is a wonderful British rampart. (*Vide* page 50 for British lake villages.)

[5] Eminent architects and antiquaries say that the stone bears marks of being cut by flint implements. *Vide* p. 50.

the place and was ever ready to impart her knowledge. The former hostel is now a boys' school.

Chalice Hill, Chalice Well, all bespeak St. Joseph and the Holy Grail. St. Joseph and his eleven anchorites lived round the sacred well, and hence the house, in whose grounds the well is, was known as the Anchorage, and later as the Anchor Inn.

There is also in Glastonbury a spot of great significance, unknown to the tourists, little known to and less realized by the inhabitants. It is approached from the High Street, between two shops opposite the Abbot's Tribunal, where the Abbot formerly dispensed justice. Great were his rights and privileges. Not only King's Officers, but even King Edward I, our great law-giver, bowed before them in person, and when on a visit to Glastonbury held an Assize at Street outside the Abbot's jurisdiction. The Tribunal, a beautiful building with lovely ceilings and a repose of its own, was lately used as Church property, being rented for Church Lads' Clubs and other parochial meetings. There it was shown to visitors, and a free exhibition of arts and crafts by living artists was carried on there. Now, the late owner, Mr. Robert Neville Grenville of Butleigh Court, has given it to the Board of Works, who are restoring it well. The way which we have to find, covered over, disturbed, and obscured, is the old way by which the monks passed from the Abbey to the Tribunal. Those who persevere in following up the passage opposite the Tribunal are rewarded. Suddenly they find themselves within the ancient walls of the Abbey. There in front of them is the Norman chapel of St. Mary, built in 1184 after the fire, on the site of the wattle Church of St. Joseph. The first man to build on to the Olde Churche was St. David of Wales, and he built to the eastward; but a most ancient inscription[6]

[6] *Vide* p. 198.

taught that he jealously put up a pillar to mark where the Olde Churche ended, and the foundation of that pillar was dug for successfully in 1921, and can be seen.[7] Standing where we are, our eyes are looking on the spot where from the time of the disciples of Christ there has been a church, now, alas, ruined, but restorable. Casting one's eyes upward to the left through the trees, one gets a glimpse of St. Michael's Tower on the Tor. Here, then, we see the site on which the first humble Christian church was built, and we see also where, one hundred years after, the wattle church had conquered, Britain was converted, and a Christian church crowned the height of pagan worship.[8] But this is not all. Without moving, we notice a tiny chapel to our right, still used as a chapel for the Royal Almshouses for Women. This chapel is dedicated to St. Patrick of Ireland, who, William of Malmesbury teaches us, was the first Abbot here, after he returned from Ireland to rule and die here. It is probably the only mediaeval chapel in England dedicated to St. Patrick; but this is not its real interest. It is something far greater. This little chapel, built by the monks for their almsfolk, was spared at the Reformation when its lofty sisters were spoiled and all but demolished. Its ancient stone altar still stands, and is used.[9] You could most easily throw a stone

[7] *Vide* p. 199.

[8] A peep extremely difficult to get now since the Abbey trustees have planted a tall privet hedge and closed some steps there, having acquired the old burial place of distinguished strangers.

[9] The slab of this altar is still older than its base. It has plainly been moved, and broken, and patched. It opens endless possibilities. It may go back to the dimmest ages of Celtic antiquity. The priceless altars offered to Glastonbury would sometimes displace others. And the monks would keep the latter sacred till wanted again as altars. One may mention that two water and metal diviners, one a professional, one an

and hit St. Joseph's Chapel. *So that from the time of
Christ's disciples, within a stone's throw of where St.
Joseph reared his first church and Christian altar, and
within the same ancient church grounds, worship in a
Christian church and at a Christian altar have never
ceased.* The little chapel of St. Patrick is now open to the
public, and is indeed a place for pilgrimage. The date of
its building is uncertain. The almshouses, to which it is
attached, were not built till 1512 by Abbot Bere, the last
Abbot but one. But the chapel is probably much older.
Standing to the north of it, one can see by looking carefully a blocked-up doorway, probably Norman, much older
than the Tudor one. And it strikes one how small the
original chapel must have been. It can hardly have been
a Gate-house Chapel. Much more likely it was a little
overflow shrine for the Irish pilgrims who flocked here in
the 12th century from Wexford via Bristol. William of
Malmesbury casually alludes in 1129 to their haunting the
place.[10] Two centuries earlier St. Dunstan was taught by
Irish monks at Glastonbury Abbey. It is extremely prob-
able that after the great fire in 1184, when the remains of
St. Patrick were placed in a silver pyramid to the south of
the altar of St. Mary's Chapel, some were placed in the
altar of St. Patrick's Chapel. There is a very big recess in
the south side of the altar.

Tempting as it is, one must not here tell the wonderful
later history of the British and Saxon church at Glastonbury, with all the illustrious names connected with it, St.
Patrick, St. David, St. Bride, St. Dunstan, and a multitude
of others. This is an attempt to state the traditions of its
earliest origin, and then to show what an accumulation

---

amateur, unknown to each other, have volunteered that a considerable amount of precious metal is under the altar and
before it, rather to the right-hand side, some feet down.

[10] To kiss St. Patrick's relics. Cap. XII.

of corroborative testimony there is from all branches and the earliest ages of the Church.[11] Archbishop Ussher and Stillingfleet both accepted the tradition, so strong both in North and South Wales and in London, that St. Paul preached in Britain. Professor Ramsay points out that there is a gap in St. Paul's history between A.D. 62 and 65.[12] St. Clement said that he preached to " the utmost bound of the West ". Tradition names Gospel Oak, near London, and the Temple of Diana, where now St. Paul's Cathedral stands, as spots where he preached.[13] A piece of Church ground at Glastonbury was called Paul's Field.[14]

In the South of England also there lingers a tradition of St. Paul's landing. Close to busy modern Portsmouth stands what was the village of Porchester, at the far end of the harbour. As its name denotes, it was a Roman Fort, and the foundations of the castle are still there. It was the chief port also of this part of the country, and was called Portus Adurnis. The modern Portsmouth was then a mud-flat, at the entrance to this busy flourishing port. Locally the traditions of this busy port remain, and there is a further tradition that St. Paul landed to the east of the present Porchester at a spot still called Paul's Grove or Paul Grove. Until lately there was a grove of ancient trees running down to the water's edge, but the trees are now nearly gone. A main road runs through what was the grove, and an oil depot occupies part of it! A few old trees on the far side of the road still linger on private ground

[11] For an account of later saints see the author's *Glastonbury, the Mother of Saints*.

[12] Archbishop Edwards of St. Asaph's *Landmarks*, p. 3.

[13] The fact that there are various Gospel Oaks in the country, deriving their name from being connected with religious processions, does not disprove the tradition. On the contrary an oak with such a tradition would be most likely to be utilized for such a procession.

[14] The origin of the name is not traced.

attached to an old house, sole tangible witnesses of the ancient tradition, and possibly of the coming of the great Apostle there. But still the name Paul's Grove lingers as a suburb of Portsmouth. (This was written before the 1939–45 War. How is it now?)

It is claimed, not without some reason, that the great monastery at Bangor was founded by St. Paul.[15] But the first seed in Britain was sown in Avalon or Glastonbury by St. Joseph of Arimathea, or other disciples of Christ.

It is fashionable to decry all legends and deny all tradition. And I have heard it stated with an air of great authority that the story of the foundation of the Church of Glastonbury by Joseph of Arimathea, or other contemporaries of Christ, was invented by the monks, and that no trace of such story can be found before William of Malmesbury recorded it.[16] Is this true, that there is no earlier record? If it were, we should remember that William was a careful and fairly critical historian, who had advantages which we no longer possess. He wrote the *Acts of the Kings of the English*, and he was invited by the

[15] The stages of British Monasticism were (1) A Village of huts within a ditch or palisade, as at Glastonbury, or a group of cells in rocks; (2) A School to train the young, as Llan Iltud about A.D. 500; (3) Hermits who by about 550 A.D. had grown common. Bangor probably passed through the two first stages, as Glastonbury did. *Vide* pp. 27 and 82.

[16] Quite recently a dignitary in Wells is stated to have gone out of his way to tell an antiquarians' party who were coming to Glastonbury next day, that the story of Our Lord's coming to Glastonbury and Priddy was entirely invented some 50 years ago by a school teacher at Priddy when writing a play for an entertainment. Unfortunately for the dignitary, there are nonagenarians alive who knew the story in their childhood, not to speak of William Blake's hymn. If one has a zest in destroying beautiful old traditions, it is a pity to invent new myths to do it. There are worthier ways of embalming oneself. The party were not pleased. (See Appendix 6.)

monks of Glastonbury to go there and write a history of their famous Abbey, which he did in A.D. 1129, revising it in 1135. He had the advantage there of a glorious library, now dispersed or destroyed, a fountain of traditions now almost dried up, and a history in stone now almost demolished. This little brochure is a very humble effort, written in a very busy life, to provide a little popular account, showing that there is a great deal of cumulative evidence, much earlier than William of Malmesbury, pointing to the very early foundation of our national Church, and of that of Glastonbury in particular. It must be borne in mind that it has never been disputed that Glastonbury is the Mother Church of Britain (all authors of weight and repute on the subject admit it). And, therefore, even authorities that do not name Glastonbury, but point to the earliest Church in Britain, frequently point to Glastonbury alone or in part.

PART III

AUTHORITIES

THE COMING OF THE DISCIPLES OF CHRIST
THE COMING OF ST. JOSEPH OF ARIMATHEA
THE COMING OF ST. PHILIP TO FRANCE
THE COMING OF ST. SIMON ZELOTES
THE COMING OF ARISTOBULUS
THE COMING OF ST. PAUL

CHAPTER 6

THE COMING OF THE DISCIPLES OF CHRIST

(1) EUSEBIUS, A.D. 260–340, Bishop of Caesarea, and Father of Ecclesiastical History, wrote: "The apostles passed beyond the ocean to the Isles called the Britannic Isles" (*De Demonstratione Evangelii*, Lib. iii). It is worthy of note that Eusebius was at the Council of Nicaea, A.D. 325, where he took a leading part. There he must have met the British bishops.

(2) ST. HILARY OF POITIERS, A.D. 300–367, wrote: "Afterwards the Apostles built several tabernacles, and through all the parts of the earth wherever it was possible to go; even in the Isles of the Ocean they built several habitations for God. (Tract. in XIV. Psalm 8. Haddan and Stubbs, Vol. 1, p. 5.) The most ancient French bishoprics claimed to have been founded by the companions of St. Joseph (*vide* Rabanus, p. 90).

(3) GILDAS THE WISE, ALBANICUS,[1] A.D. 425–512, who was driven by Saxon pirates from the island of Steepholme, near the modern Weston-super-Mare, and took refuge in Glastonbury Abbey, and became a monk there, till he got permission to resume his anchorite life in an adjacent cell, where he founded a little oratory to the Undivided and Blessed Trinity on the site of what is undoubtedly Street parish church, which has a double dedication to the Holy

[1] Alford (*Fides Regia Britannica*, p. 68) under Anno 73 gives three Gildases: (1) Gildas Cambrius who flourished A.D. 73, and is said to have translated Brutus's prayer to Diana into Latin; (2) St. Gildas (the Wise) Albanicus (A.D. 425–512, here quoted); and (3) Gildas Badonicus (A.D. 516–570). *Vide* later, pp. 97, 98 n.

Trinity and St. Gildas (the latter almost forgotten). He says, " Christ, the True Sun, afforded His light, the knowledge of His precepts, to our island in the last year, *as we know*, of Tiberius Caesar " (*De excidio Britanniæ*, Sec. 8, p. 25). *This was in* A.D. 37, *four years after the crucifixion*. This is the date of the persecution of the Church by Saul of Tarsus, when " they were all scattered abroad except the Apostles ", and it fits in with the story of St. Joseph and others being put in a boat. The " as we know " has a special significance arising from one steeped in the lore of Glastonbury. Eusebius (*Eec. Hist.*, Bk. 2, Cap. 2 and 3) confirms the fact of Tiberius's protection of the Church. Thus Christianity spread rapidly.

(4) ST. AUGUSTINE, writing A.D. 600 to Pope Gregory,[2] shows how the belief of the founding of the Church of St. Mary at Glastonbury by the Disciples of Christ had grown into something more: " In the western confines of Britain there is a certain royal island of large extent, surrounded by water, abounding in all the beauties of nature and necessaries of life. In it *the first neophytes of Catholic Law*, God beforehand acquainting them, found a Church constructed by no human art, but by the Hands of Christ Himself, for the salvation of His people. The Almighty has made it manifest by many miracles and mysterious visitations that He continues to watch over it as sacred to Himself, and to Mary, the Mother of God." This is remarkable testimony as to the apostolic origin of a church that would have nothing to do with the same St. Augustine, who replied to him through Dianothus, its bishop, who was also Abbot of Bangor, " Be it known and declared that we all, individually and collectively, are in all humility

---

[2] *Epistolae ad Gregorium Papam*. The Saxon Priest B. quotes it in his very early life of St. Dunstan about A.D. 1000, of which William of Malmesbury saw a copy at Glastonbury. See also Spelman's *Concilia*, pp. 5, 108, 109.

prepared to defer to the Church of God, and to the Bishop
of Rome, and to every sincere and godly Christian, so far
as to love every one according to his degree, in perfect
charity, and to assist them all by word and in deed in
becoming the children of God. But as for any other
obedience, we know of none that he whom you term Pope,
or Bishop of Bishops, can demand. The deference we have
mentioned we are ready to pay to him as to every other
Christian, but in all other respects our obedience is due to
the jurisdiction of the Bishop of Caerlon, who is alone
under God our ruler to keep us right in the way of salvation.[3]

St. Augustine's testimony is all the more wonderful since
Bede, A.D. 740, stated: " The Britons are contrary to the
whole Roman world, and enemies to the Roman customs,
not only in their Mass, but in their tonsure.[4] . . . The
Britons, though they for the most part as a nation hate and
oppose the English nation, and wrongfully and from
wicked lewdness set themselves against the appointed
custom of the whole Catholic Church," etc. (Bede, Bk. 2,
C. 23). Bede also complained, writing A.D. 715, that the
Britons had refused to convert the English; and that when
the latter were converted and adopted Roman customs,
" the Britons still persist in their errors, halting and turn-
ing aside from the true path, expose their head without a

[3] Spelman's *Concilia*, pp. 108, 109; Haddan and Stubbs, Vol.
1, p. 122. Haddan and Stubbs take this reply from Spelman.
Spelman got it from a MS. of Mr. Peter Mostyn who thought
it to be ancient, or a copy of an ancient one. Two copies exist:
(1) Cotton MSS., Cleop., E.1; (2) Claud A.VIII, 76.
[4] The Romans shaved the top of their head only, and let
the hair grow round. The Celts shaved the whole front of the
head, and left the hair at the back. Easterns shaved the whole
head. Theodore of Tarsus was not allowed to be ordained
Bishop, and was sent to Britain in A.D. 668, till his hair had
grown and Roman tonsure had been performed.

crown, and keep the feast of Christ apart from the fellow-
ship of the Church of Christ "[5] (Bede, Bk. V, C. 22–23).
In view of this antagonism St. Augustine's testimony is
wonderful.

(5) It may be pardonable here to enumerate the points
on which the British Church differed from the Roman,
differences quite sufficient to suggest a differing origin.
Professor Lumby in his *History of the Creeds*, Camb.,
1873, says on this subject: "The oriental character of some
of the observances of the early British Church points
directly to this conclusion "—viz., that when Irenaeus,
Bishop of Lyons in 177 (himself an Eastern Churchman,
pupil of St. Polycarp, brought up at the feet of St. John),
spoke of the Churches of the Kelts, he was including the
Church in Britain. The British Church was part of the
Gallican Church, which derived from the East, and not
from Rome. Haddan and Stubbs enumerate seven differences (Vol. L, Appendix D, pp. 152–155) as follows:

(*a*) *Date of Easter*. This difference stresses independence
rather than different origin. From the Council of Nicea,
A.D. 315, till at any rate 455, they used the same cycle. In
458 Rome changed. In 597 St. Augustine found the Britons
using the old cycle.

(*b*) *Baptism*. Probably one immersion; not three. Both
Churches had Chrism and Confirmation. St. Patrick in his
letter to Coroticus mentions that he had undergone both.

(*c*) *Tonsure* different from Greek and Roman. The
British tonsure was Druidical, which causes speculation as
to whether Druidical monasteries came over wholesale to
Christianity about A.D 167. The Bretons also kept it. A
Coly of Saxons at Bayeux had before 590 copied it from

---

[5] Abbot Ceolfrid, in his letter to King Naiton of the Picts,
A.D. 710 (Bede's *Eccl. Hist.*) urges conformity to Roman custom
in the tonsure, but admits that "the Catholic Church does not
use one and the same form of tonsure throughout the world".

the Bretons. The Council of Toledo IV, A.D. 633 condemned it.

(*d*) *Mass*. Peculiar ritual. A multiplicity of Collects.

(*e*) *Ordination*. Peculiar ritual. Certain Lections taken from a British Latin version. The anointing of the hands of deacons; the anointing of heads of priests and bishops, of the bishops twice; prayer at the giving of the stole to the deacons; delivering of the Gospel to deacons; *investing* the priest with the stole.

(*f*) *Bishops*. The consecration of bishops by *a single bishop*, as in the cases of Dubricius and Teilo, and in the later Irish Church.

(*g*) *Churches and Monasteries*. A peculiar way of consecrating.

(6) CHARTERS. I will not press the point of every charter of all the early kings, British or Saxon (including those of Ina and Edgar) calling Glastonbury the first church in the kingdom, and cradle of Christ's religion in Britain, founded by Christ's disciples, as the genuineness of some at least of the charters is suspect. But above has been quoted early Roman, Eastern and British authority.

(7) NICEPHORUS, Patriarch of Constantinople, and Byzantine historian, A.D. 758–820. Michael Alford the Jesuit in his *Fides Regia Britannica* under Anno Christ. 47, Peter 3, Caractaci Regis, 3, Claudii, Imp. 5, wrote: "And speaking carefully there can scarcely be a doubt that one of the Apostles preached there [Britain] if there should be any hesitation in naming the Apostle" (later he definitely names St. Simon Zelotes). Alford then quotes Nicephorus, speaking of the Dispersion of the Apostles: "One reached Egypt and Libya, another reached the extreme regions of the Ocean, and the British Isles" (Nicephorus, Lib. 1, cap. 1).

(8) FLAVIUS DEXTER. Cressy in his *Church History of Brittany* (cap. V) quotes him thus: "In the one and fortieth

year of Christ St. James returning out of Spain visited
Gaule, Brittany [Britain] and the Towns of the Venetians
where he preached the Gospel, and so came back to Jerusalem to consult with the Blessed Virgin, and St. Peter
about matters of very great weight and importance." The
statement that St. James, great among the Apostles as first
Bishop of Jerusalem, and kinsman of Our Lord, visited
Britain five years after the earliest date given for St.
Joseph's coming, is of interest. In the year named we know
from Acts XI that St. Peter was in Jerusalem contending
for the reception of Gentiles into the Church, as he was
five years later, when St. James presided there at the first
Church Council, which dealt with the same subject. It
must be remembered that at four Church Councils it was
held that St. Joseph founded the British Church immediately after the Passing of Christ, before St. James founded
the Spanish.

(9) RABANUS. Maurus, Archbishop of Mayence, A.D.
776–856. *Life of St. Mary Magdelene.* This claims in the
Prologue to be " according to the accounts that our fathers
have left us in their writings ".

It is highly important to consider the stream of saints
to the West so learnedly set forth in Taylor's *Coming of
the Saints.* Rabanus tells us French and Spanish traditions.
Both nations tell of the occupants of the boat without oars
and without sails travelling down the Mediterranean to
Marseilles; amongst others, the three Marys—St. Mary
Magdalen, Mary wife of Cleophas or Alphaeus, and Mary
Salome wife of Zebedee and mother of St. James and St.
John—Martha, Lazarus, Maximin, Trophinnus, Eutropius,
Marcella the maid who was with Martha at her death,
Sara the black woman, and Joseph of Arimathea (who
passed on). There are traces of these all along the Rhone
Valley right up to the coast of Brittany at Morlaix.
Rabanus tells us Trophinnus became the first Bishop of

Arles, Eutropius of Aquitaine. It is interesting that the *Jewish Encyclopaedia*, under Arles, says that the earliest Jewish settlers at Arles came in a boat which had been deserted by its captain. (Hence, probably, no sails, no oars.) Drennalus, first Bishop of Treguier and a disciple of St. Joseph, preached the Gospel at Morlaix. Maximain and St. Mary Magdalen went to Aix, where Mary lived and died, and of which Maximain became first Bishop. Parmenas, St. Martha and Marcella went to Avignon and Arles, and finally Martha settled and died at Tarascon, and so on. The whole country breathes memories of these saints. St. Joseph did not remain there. St. Lazarus, said to have been first Bishop of Cyprus before the voyage in the boat, settled and died at Marseilles, where his 1st-century church is shown today. This book of Rabanus was in the catalogue of Glastonbury Abbey books in A.D. 1248, so doubtless William of Malmesbury saw it.

(10) FASTES. *Episcoporum* (Vol. ii, 104). These give the 10th-century Aquitaine tradition that St. Martial and his father and mother, Marcellus and Elizabeth, St. Zacchaeus and St. Joseph of Arimathea arrived at Limoges in the 1st century. St. Joseph does not remain. Rabanus's evidence quoted above that St. Joseph preached at Morlaix on the coast of Brittany opposite Britain, and the evidence of the Fastes *Episcoporum* that he also preached at Limoges and did not remain, and all the above French church evidence fits in with Cardinal Baronius's evidence about the journey by boat of St. Joseph and his companions to Marseilles, and to William of Malmesbury's evidence that St. Joseph was sent from France by St. Philip to Britain.

CHAPTER 7

THE COMING OF ST. JOSEPH OF ARIMATHEA

(1) CARDINAL BARONIUS,[1] the great Church historian, and most learned librarian to the Vatican, in his *Ecclesiastical Annals*, on which he spent 30 years, under the year A.D. 35, states that in that year Joseph of Arimathea, Lazarus,[2] Mary, Martha, Marcella,[3] their maid, and Maximin, a disciple, were put by the Jews into a boat without sails and without oars,[4] and floated down the Mediterranean and landed at Marseilles,[5] and thence Joseph and his company

---

[1] *Annales Ecclesiastice*, 1601 edition, Tom. 1, f 327. Baronius was a most careful historian. He wrote "Melius silentium quam mendacium veris admixtum" (Better silence than a lie mixed with truth) when writing about St. Catherine of Alexandria.

[2] Among the ancient British Triads there is a Triad of Lazarus, the only ancient writing about Lazarus apart from Holy Scripture. The French traditions of Lazarus and his companions clustering round Marseilles fit in with the British.

[3] Jacobus Valderius, in his *De dignitate regum et regnorum Hispaniæ* says that it was Marcella who cried out to Our Lord, "Blessed is the womb that bare Thee", and that Maximin was the man blind from birth whom Our Lord healed (Cap. 6, Sec. 58).

[4] It is most interesting that in *Le Sant Graal* the memory of this form of voyaging had got so associated with St. Joseph that the poem accredited him with coming to Britain "Sans aviron, et sans gouvernal, ne ongues n'i ot voile fors le giron de sa cemise", and that this obliging shirt brought St. Joseph, the Holy Grail and 150 people to our shores! (Eugene Hucher's edition, Paris, 1877, II, p. 49).

[5] It is an amazing fact that to this day all the gipsies of France make an annual pilgrimage to Saintes Maries de la Mer at the mouth of the Rhine, where the barque of Lazarus is

92

crossed into Britain, and preached the Gospel there, and finally died there. The annals quote *The Acts of Magdalen* for the voyage to Marseilles and an ancient MS. history of England in the Vatican for St. Joseph's mission to England and his death there. William of Malmesbury says that St. Philip sent twelve missionaries from France to Britain, of whom the leader was St. Joseph of Arimathea, and that the King gave them Ynys-vitrin, or Avalon, or Glastonbury, and twelve Hides of land.

(2) "THE RECOGNITIONS OF CLEMENT"—a 2nd-century document tainted with Ebionite errors, probably based on an account by St. Clement of Rome (so Rufinus, who translated it in A.D. 410, thought) describes St. Barnabus and St. Clement going to Caesarea and finding there, among others, SS. Peter, Lazarus, the Holy Women, and St. Joseph of Arimathea! Here we find not only St. Joseph but some of the group whom we find later in the boat. It may be that they started from Caesarea on their voyage.

(3) DOMESDAY BOOK contains this entry: "The Church of Glastonbury has in its own ville twelve Hides of land, *which have never paid tax*" (Domesday Survey folio p. 249*b*). *Domesday Book* was certainly only written for one purpose, and it is a very suggestive confirmation of the early grant of twelve Hides by Arviragus to St. Joseph of Arimathea.[5a]

(4) "THE PSEUDO-GOSPEL OF NICODEMUS," an Oriental MS., generally attributed to the 4th century, but which Tischendorf thinks to be very early 2nd century, and Dr. Rendel Harris thinks "very early", towards the end states that St. Joseph suffered persecution.

---

said to have come on shore, to venerate the relics of three holy women and his companions, Marie Salome, Marie Jacobe, and in especial Sara, their black servant (*vide Morning Post*, May 28, 1923).

[5a] *Vide* p. 10.

(5) MAELGWYN OF AVALON or MELCHINUS, the uncle of St. David, and "who was before Merlin", about A.D. 540, wrote (in his *Historia de Rebus Britannicis*, which John Leland records seeing in the Glastonbury Abbey Library in 1534. Leland held Henry VIII's licence to search for ancient records in all cathedrals, colleges, abbeys and priories. He was the "King's antiquary"): "The Isle of Avalon greedy of burials . . . received thousands of sleepers, among whom Joseph de Marmore[6] from Aramathea by name, entered his perpetual sleep. And he lies in a bifurcated line next the southern angle of the oratory made of circular wattles by 13 inhabitants of the place[7] over the powerful adorable Virgin. Joseph had with him moreover in his sarcophagus, two white and silver cruets filled with the blood and sweat of the prophet Jesus.[8] When his

[6] It sounds as if St. Joseph was known as of Marmore before he was known as of Arimathea. Mr. W. J. King, of Canonical House, The Liberty, Wells, suggests that Marmore may be Marmore in the Island of Scio off Smyrna, or Marmorica, the coastal district west of Egypt. He also suggests, if this last interpretation be right, that it might account for the Egyptian character of the Chalice Well at Glastonbury, which eminent Egyptologists have mentioned. Mr. Harding-King has himself made archaeological excavations in Marmorica.

[7] The reference to thirteen inhabitants is most interesting. St. Joseph had twelve companions. The thirteenth may have been a native expert.

[8] On several buildings put up by Abbot Bere there is a design of a rough cross between two covered vessels with handles. It is generally said that this is a canting rebus of two beer-jugs and a cross, and has reference to the Abbot's name. It is hard to be believed. Both Mr. Bligh Bond and the author have separately come to the conclusion that these vessels represent the cruets with the blood and the sweat of Our Lord, and that this was adopted as an emblem by the Abbey. To support this it appears in 15th-century glass in the south window of the sanctuary of the parish church on a background

sarcophagus shall be opened it will be seen whole, and untouched in the future, and will be open to the whole world. From then neither water, nor dew of heaven, shall fail those inhabiting this most noble island. For much time before the Day of Judgment these things shall be open in Josaphat and declared to the living."[9] It is rash to assert that the two cruets here referred to are merely another version of the Holy Grail story. Here we can trace the cruet story back to Maelgwyn or Melchinus in speaking of St. Joseph's burial. If Gildas Badonicus, A.D. 516–570, wrote *The Acts of the Illustrious King Arthur* we have a reference to the Holy Grail about the same date, for we read: "In the search for a vessel which they there call the Holy Grail it is related almost in the beginning, where Galaat, a white knight, shows to his son Lancelot the mystery of a certain wonderful shield, which he committed to him to carry, which no one else without great damage could carry even for one day."[10] Not till the 12th century does the story of the Holy Grail appear in its vigour, when in Henry II's reign it appears simultaneously in Britain and France. Walter Mape, a great figure in Henry II's court,

---

with drops of colourless liquid, and in some cases the vessels appear without handles. The abbey farms and other buildings bear emblems.

[9] *John of Glastonbury*, Hearne's small edition, 1726, p. 55. Capgrave's *De Sancto Joseph at Aramathia*. The *Magna Tabula of Glastonbury* at Haworth Castle. Ussher, *Antiq.*, p. 12, 1687 edition; a thick vellum Cottonian MS.; *Flores Historiarum* (Master of the Rolls series), 1890, p. 127. John Leland, the great antiquary, specially mentions seeing Melchinus's book in Glastonbury Abbey library shortly before the Dissolution.

[10] The so-called Emperor Theodorius' *De Sancto Joseph ab Aramathia* (from which William of Malmesbury makes long extracts in his Cap. 1) also mentions the Holy Grail, which may help to date the book.

embalmed it in England. He had been parish priest at
Westbury in Wiltshire, and Canon of Salisbury, both
places within easy reach of Glastonbury, before he became
Archdeacon of Oxford. The earliest references on the
Continent are by Chretien de Troyes, Wolfram von Eschen-
bach, and Robert le Boron. De Troyes wrote *Les Contes
del Graal* from a book given him by Comte Phillippe de
Flandres, 1185–89. In 1198–1210 Wolfram wrote the
German story *Parsifal*. He quotes Ghretien, but repudiates
his story, and says that his own came from Kyot le
Provencal, le Chanteur. This is a lost French source, probably Breton; Robert le Boron wrote about 1204. We cannot
forget the intimate intercourse between Britain and
Brittany, and the ties of their royal houses. But the lays
of the Holy Grail have Glastonbury's two stories of St.
Joseph and King Arthur inextricably mixed. When
Arthur's body was found in 1190–1191 the two stories, as
given to him by the Comte de Flandres, awoke and the
troubadours carried them in their lays all over Europe (see
Appendix 4).

Was the book referred to above by de Troyes Walter
Mape's or some much earlier book? Robert le Boron says
that the story was first told by " great Clerks ". This shows
an ecclesiastical source. M. Paulin Paris, who spent forty
years on the subject, is of opinion that the story came first
from a Welsh monk or hermit who lived in the 8th century.
The Acts of the Illustrious King Arthur referred to above,
relating the search of Sir Lancelot for the Holy Grail, also
speaks of a hermit called Waleran, who explains the
mystery of a fountain which continuously changes taste
and colour. John of Glastonbury[11] gives the already quoted
passage from Maelgwyn or Melchinus. This passage is also
found added in the margin of the Cambridge MS. of

[11] Page 55, Hearne's smaller edition.

William of Malmesbury's *De Antiquitate Glastoniæ* in a very old handwriting. Vincent Belovacensis in his *Speculum Historiale*, Lib. 23, cap. 147, under the year A.D. 719, also tells of a hermit in Britain who had a vision of St. Joseph of Arimathea and the Holy Grail. There is some persistently lingering memory of a hermit in connection with the Holy Grail. The date of the earliest history of the Holy Grail is in dispute. It has been stated under the title of " Le Seynt Graal " as A.D. 717. M. Paulin Paris in his *Romans de la Table Ronde* (Vol. 1, p. 91) strongly supports this date after spending forty years on the question. Helinand, a monk of the French Abbey of Fromond, who died about 1219, in his *Chronicle*, which ended with the year 1209, quotes under the year A.D. 717 the writing of a hermit in Britain, who had a vision that year of St. Joseph and the Graal. In this French book the amazing claim was made that the Hermit's Latin writing was made by no mortal hand. This is especially interesting, for exactly the same type of claim was made in one part of William of Malmesbury's *De Antiquitate Glastoniæ* that the wattle church was built by no mortal hand. There is a tinge of the divine about Glastonbury and things connected with it. Is it the memory of a Presence? For further remarks about the origin of the Lays of King Arthur see Appendix 4.

(6) "THE VICTORY OF AURELIUS AMBROSIUS." A.D. 516–570, GILDAS BADONICUS. This book is now lost. Aurelius Ambrosius, or Ambrosius Aurelianus, British Emperor, "Prince of the Sanctuary", was almost certainly the son of the British Emperor, Constantine, and grandson of Constantine the Great, brother of Uther Pendragon, and uncle of King Arthur. Geoffrey of Monmouth (about A.D. 1135) refers to this book as written by Gildas (Bohn's edition, p. 155). Professor W. A. S. Hewins in his *Royal Saints of Britain*, p. 52, calls Ambrosius " the connecting

link between the Roman Empire and modern Britain . . .
one of the greatest figures in British history and romance
—the last of the Romans . . . the protagonist against the
Saxons . . . the Emrys of the Welsh—but with all that a
perfectly historical character ". Aurelius and his brother
Uther Pendragon, the father of Arthur, after the murder
of their elder brother Constans, and the usurpation of his
crown by Vortigern, fled into Brittany, and were brought
up as princes by the king there. On his return Aurelius
burned Vortigern, and took the crown, defeated Hengist,
and restored the kingdom to the British. Sir Henry Spelman also in his *Concilia* assigns this book to Gildas, and
quotes from it thus: "Another Gildas, Albanicus,[12]
strongly supports him [Gildas Badonicus] in this opinion,
who in the book of the *Victory of Aurelius Ambrosius*
plainly asserts that Britain received the gospel in the time
of the Emperor Tiberius, and he adds also that Joseph of
Arimathea was sent (after the dispersion of the Disciples)
to Britain by Philip the Apostle, about the year of Our
Lord 63 and that he himself stayed here all his life, and
along with his companions laid the foundations of the
Christian religion."[13] There is little doubt that Gildas saw
this book in Glastonbury Abbey library, and that some six
centuries later (1135) Geoffrey of Monmouth at least heard
of it from his friend William of Malmesbury, resident
there. Both William and Geoffrey dedicated books to the
same patron, Robert Duke of Gloucester.

Professor W. A. S. Hewins, in his *Royal Saints of Britain*,
gives a whole section to Ambrosius Aurelianus, pp. 52–56.
He says " It is generally accepted that Ambrosius was the

[12] Spelman and Alford differ as to which of the second and
third Gildases is Albanicus or Badonicus.

[13] Here then again is very early testimony, long before
William of Malmesbury, about St. Philip sending St. Joseph
to Britain; apparently both Gildases testified to it.

son of a descendant of Constantine" (the Great). Professor
Rhys thinks him the son of Juventus or Jovin. And the
name Jovin is constant in his descendants. He shows reason
to think that Ambrosius was a son of Jovin by a daughter
of Constantine, and that he was King of the Cotswolds.
He claims that Mons Badonicus, where the great battle
was fought, was Bown Hill near Woodchester, overlooking
the Severn Valley. There the Saxons were defeated in 490.
It is quite natural that Gildas Badonicus should write the
life of a hero of his neighbourhood.

(7) "THE ACTS OF THE ILLUSTRIOUS KING ARTHUR." This
book is also lost. It is quoted by several authors. The
passage quoted below is found added in a very old hand,
as from this book, in the margin of the Cambridge MS. of
William of Malmesbury's *De Antiquitate Glastoniæ*, Cap.
2. John of Glastonbury also quotes it (p. 55, Hearne's small
edition). So does Capgrave, in his *De Sancto Joseph at
Arimathea* (1393–1464). John Capgrave was Principal of
the Augustinian Friars in England. He received Henry VI
at his Friary at Lynn in Norfolk in 1466. He was full of
Glastonbury lore. Probably these lost books were in Glastonbury's wonderful Library, which awakened John
Leland's admiration in 1534, before the Dissolution. When
one thinks of the ravages of the Saxons and Danes, the
wars between King Stephen and the Empress Maud, the
Wars of the Roses, various rebellions, and the Dissolution
of the Monasteries, the wonder is not at what is lost, but
at what has survived. The authorship of the book is attributed to Gildas (A.D. 516–570). John of Glastonbury certainly knew the books of Glastonbury Abbey. Capgrave
must at least have corresponded with the monks of that
Abbey before he wrote his treatise on St. Joseph. The
passage is as follows: " The book of *The Acts of the Illustrious King Arthur* testifies that in the quest of a certain
Knight called Lancelot of the Lake made by the Com-

panions of the Round Table (viz., where a certain hermit revealed to Waleran the mystery of a certain fountain that changed its taste and colour frequently) [? the Chalice Well] which miracle should not cease until there should come a great lion, which also should have his neck bound with great chains; that Joseph of Arimathea a noble decurio with his son called Joseph and several others came into Greater Britain which is now called England, and there finished his life."[14]

(8) EMPEROR THEODOSIUS. *De Sancto Joseph at Arimathea.* John of Glastonbury at the end of the 14th century and John Capgrave (1393–1464) both give the same long extract from a book which they claimed that the Emperor Theodosius (A.D. 379–395) found in Pilate's Pretorium in Jerusalem. It is only possible to summarize it, whatever the book was. It was evidently composed after the earliest *Book of the Holy Graal*, which it quotes, whatever date that may be. It narrates the miraculous, and much is palpably absurd. But to leave it out altogether is to lose some of the atmosphere around this story and its statement about events in Britain. It states that immediately after the crucifixion the Jews sought to arrest St. Joseph, Nicodemus and others. The others hid, but St. Joseph and Nicodemus went boldly to the Jews. St. Joseph was imprisoned in a windowless cell, Nicodemus allowed to depart. The seals of Annas and Caiaphas were fixed to the lock of the cell, and a guard stationed. On the Sabbath the Jews met to consider how to put Joseph to death. They sent for him but the cell was empty, and St. Joseph was found in Arimathea. The Sanhedrim sent him a

[14] So we have Gildas Badonicus writing in two separate books (both, alas, lost) that St. Joseph came to Britain and died here. One wonders whether Lord Bath's library at Longleat, which has valuable Glastonbury MSS., by any chance has these two books.

message of repentance and good-will by seven men. (This
is quite contrary to the simple natural narrative told by
Baronius.[15] Joseph rejoiced, came and declared that Our
Lord had appeared to him in a vision while in prison. St.
Joseph had asked to be shown the Tomb where he had
buried Him, and Our Lord led him there, and showed him
the sindony in which he had wrapped Him, and the face-
cloth. Then he adored Him, and Our Lord led him to his
house at Arimathea, and forbade him to leave it for forty
days. After this St. Joseph went to St. Philip to be taught,
and with his son Josephes was baptized by him. Later St.
John, while evangelizing Ephesus, made him Paranymphos
(guardian)[16] to the Blessed Virgin Mary. And he was
present with St. Philip and other disciples at her assumption, and immediately preached through divers regions
what he had seen and heard from Our Lord and the Blessed
Virgin, converting and baptizing many. Fifteen years after
the assumption, along with his son Josephes, whom Our
Lord had consecrated Bishop in Sarath[17] (Saraz) he came
to Philip the Apostle in the Gauls. (This is the third
mention of association with St. Philip.)[18] He converted and

[15] But it is the exaggeration of Baronius's statement from
the early Vatican MS. and from the early 2nd century (*Pseudo-
Gospel of Nicodemus*) that St. Joseph shared in the persecution of the earliest Christians.

[16] Strictly the bridesmaid, or the friend who in the East
conducts the bride to the bridegroom. The Cotton MS. Titus
A.XIX, ff. 18–19, tells the same tale. *Vide* pp. 42 and 71. St.
John and St. Joseph were alone called Paranymphos to the
Blessed Virgin.

[17] This version of Saraz is interesting, and suggests an
Eastern origin. In Yiddish the modern Jew pronounces all his
diphthongs as S. For instance, Sabbath is Shobbas, Talith is
Talis, and so on.

[18] However exaggerated the story became in the course of
time, there is the same basic fact which William of Malmesbury told later—that St. Philip sent St. Joseph to Britain.

baptized many there. St. Philip then sent him to Britain
as head of twelve (of whom Josephes was one) to preach
the Gospel. Six hundred and more men and women
accompanied him (as is to be read in the book of the Holy
Graal) under a vow. All but 150 broke it, who by God's
command crossed the sea on Joseph's shirt, on an Easter
night, and arrived in the morning.[19] The others repented,
and God sent them a ship made by King Solomon, which
had survived, and came the same day to their companions
along with a certain Prince of the Medas by name Vacion
(elsewhere Nacion) whom Joseph had formerly baptized
in Saraz, along with Mordrai a king of that city. To
Mordrai Our Lord appeared in a vision showing His hands
and feet, and pierced side. And on Nacion's enquiry who
had done these things to Him he was told "a perfidious
King of North Wales who imprisoned his servant Joseph,
preaching in those parts, denying him necessary food."
(This is very reminiscent of the words to Saul of Tarsus:
"I am Jesus Whom thou persecutest.") Our Lord charged
him to go to North Wales and deliver St. Joseph. King
Mordrai obeyed and went with an army and Duke Maxim,
and killed the King of North Wales, and released Joseph
and his companions. After this, in the year 63 Joseph, with
Josephes and ten other companions, *traversing Britain* over
which Arviragus reigned, preached Christ faithfully. The
King refused to leave the faith of his fathers, but because
of their long journey, and quiet life, he gave them a certain
island called Inswytryn (Innys Witryn), that is the Glassy
Isle, on the borders of his realm, surrounded with woods
and scrub and marshes, to dwell in.

After a very short time the aforesaid saints living in the
same wild place, were told in a vision by the Archangel

---

[19] St. Patrick also is said to have crossed on his shirt from
Ireland to Padstow in Cornwall! But this does not make St.
Patrick and his work less real.

St. Gabriel to build a church in a spot revealed to them in honour of the Blessed Mother of God, the ever Virgin Mary. Obedient to the heavenly admonition they compiled a certain chapel with circular walls of twisted twigs in the thirty-first year after Our Lord's passion, *and the fifteenth after the glorious Virgin's assumption, that is in the same year in which they came to St. Philip the Apostle in Gaul, and were sent by him to Britain,* a tabernacle of no beauty indeed, but much adorned by the grace of God. And since this was the first church in this region the Son of God endowed it with greater dignity by personally dedicating it to the honour of His Mother.

These twelve saints carrying out in the same place their duties vowed to God and the Blessed Virgin, by vigils, fasts, and prayers received the necessaries of life. Struck by the holiness of their lives, two Kings, though pagans (Marius, son of Arviragus, and Coel, son of Marius), gave to each one hide of land whence the name XII Hides. In the course of a few years these saints left the prison of the flesh, among whom also St. Joseph was buried, and placed *in a bifurcated line next the said oratory.*

The same place then began to be a hiding place for wild beasts, which had been the habitation of saints, until it pleased the Blessed Virgin that her Oratory should return to the memory of the faithful. The book is plainly fantastic and miracle-claiming. I have translated it, and summarized it, keeping as near the language of the original as that permits, because it is interesting as emphasizing the association with St. Philip, also the Nacion and Mordrai of the Grail stories, explaining who they were, and how they came in.[20] It tells how much happened in the year of arrival in Britain, and I think that it confirms

[20] How firmly the Arimathean tradition was believed is shown by the number of the earliest printed books on this subject.

and puts in chronological order a visit of St. Joseph to
Wales before he came to Glastonbury where he built the
first church in Britain. (Crewkerne in Somerset has a tradition that St. Joseph built a cell there on his way to Glastonbury.) Whatever the date of this book, it lies between some
early form of the Graal story and William of Malmesbury,
for a very great deal of William's first chapter is word for
word from this. William had the run of the Glastonbury
Library.

The name Saraz, which comes in often in the St. Joseph
story, puzzles many people. Sarum, the old name for
Salisbury, might be a clue. More likely it has some connection with the word "Saracen", a name connected with
early Jewish immigrants to this country. Polwhele in his
History of Cornwall (Falmouth, 1803) tells that the oldest
smelting places there were called "Jews' houses". There
is a tradition that Jews worked with pick-axes of holm,
box, and hartshorn (such are sometimes found among
rubble). "Jews' houses", "Jews' tin", "Jews' leavings",
"attall" and "attall Saracen", "Jews' pieces", "Jews'
works", were common phrases in Polwhele's day. There
were many Jewish colonies in the West.

Some portions of the foregoing are copied word for word
into William of Malmesbury's *De Antiquitate Glastoniæ*
(Chapter I), the only difference being that there he does not
gives names to St. Joseph and the three Kings. But earlier
in the same chapter he has said of the missionary band,
"Their leader, it is said, was Philip's dearest friend, Joseph
of Arimathea, who buried the Lord." The unnamed
Arviragus he describes as "the barbaric King", but much
later in his thirty-third chapter, William writes, "It is to
be remembered that three pagan Kings, Arviragus, Marius
and Coillus, conveyed twelve portions of land to the twelve
Disciples of Philip and James in the year of Our Lord's
Incarnation 63, and it is from this that the name 'Twelve

Hides' originated."[21] Whatever was the origin of the extraordinary book, it must have been later than King Coel, grandson of King Arviragus, and apparently than King Lucius, since it speaks of the Oratory returning to the memory of the faithful, i.e. the reconversion of Britain. Its exaggerations do not destroy the tradition which they obscure. It is of special interest that the book corroborates Maelgwyn's statement of the burial of St. Joseph " in lines bifurcata " *next* St. Mary's Chapel. Are they two independent statements? If not, which is first? Maelgwyn wrote about A.D. 540. This book claims to have been "found" between A.D. 379 and 395.

(9) WELSH EVIDENCE: (*a*) ILID. St. Joseph of Arimathea in the Welsh account of his having brought Christianity to Britain is always called " Ilid ". Why, has always been a puzzle. With diffidence I will suggest what may be a solution. The word " Ilu " is found at Babylon as the equivalent of the Hebrew Elohim, God. Jah-Elohim, God, becomes Jaum-Ilu; Jacob, Joseph, Israel, become Yakub-Ilu, Yasub-Ilu, Sar-Ili. (On the stele of Manepta in Egypt, Israel becomes Isra-Ilu.) Joseph or Yasub means " he who adds ". Does the full name Joseph-Ilu therefore mean " God's man who adds ", " God's rich man ", " God's Joseph "? In a strange land, the Yasub or Joseph might

[21] It should be noted that this book also says that St. Joseph was paranymphos to the Blessed Virgin Mary; that he and his son Josephes, afterwards Bishop of Sanas, were under instruction by St. Philip, and afterwards baptized by him; that after the Assumption of the Blessed Virgin, at which both St. Joseph and St. Philip were present, St. Joseph immediately taught what he had learned from Our Lord and the Blessed Virgin, and converted many; and that fifteen years later he went to St. Philip in France, and then evangelized Wales; was imprisoned and returned to traverse Britain, and was given the twelve Hides of Glastonbury by King Arviragus, and built the wattle church there in A.D. 65.

easily be dropped, and Ilid might well be a Welsh variant of Ilu or Ili.

(b) THE ACHAU SAINT PRYDAIN. *Genealogies of the Saints of Britain* say that "There came with Bran the Blessed from Rome Arwystli Hen (Aristobulus the aged), Ilid Cyndaf (Chief or Head), men of Israel, Maw or Mawan, son of Cyndaf."

(c) THE IOLO MSS. refer to Cyndaf coming with Garmon (pp. 100 and 102). The same MSS. tell in the Genealogy of Jestyn ap Gwrgant, Prince of Glamorgan in the 11th century, how Eurgain wife (daughter) of Caractacus or Caradoc sent for Ilid, " of the land of Israel ", from Rome to Britain to assist her in conversion of the British. "This Ilid is called in the lections of his life Joseph. He became principal teacher of the Christian faith to the Welsh, and introduced good order into Cor Eurgain, which Eurgain had established for 12 Saints near the Church now called Llantwit." *He afterwards went to Glastonbury* " where he died and was buried, and Ina, King of that country, raised a large Church over his grave "[22] (Iolo MSS., p. 7). Iolo was a faithful transcriber of MSS. The MSS. that he transcribed embalmed ancient traditions (*vide* Baring Gould's *Lives of Welsh Saints* 1, p. 198). Baring Gould (Vol. VIII, pp. 295 and 300) says that Ilid was the patron saint of Llan Ilid in Gwent. A house in that part is called Tre-Bran, and is supposed to confirm the connection of Ilid or St. Joseph with this place. Many Grail stories speak of St. Joseph going to Wales first. It is even possible that he arrived at Wirral (Weary All) Hill, Glastonbury, by land via Crewkerne, where there is a tradition that he founded a cell.

[22] The remains of King Ina's church at Glastonbury Abbey, built in A.D. 700, have been excavated in recent years, but, alas, have been covered up again. Association is one of the most powerful things in life. Tens of thousands might have been thrilled by them. Now, no one sees them.

(*d*) GESTYN CEIRIOG in the Cwydd to St. Mary Magdelene calls St. Joseph Ilid (Llanover MS., B. 1, p. 630, and Cardiff MS. 26, p. 99).

(*e*) SAYINGS OF THE WISE. One of these says, "Hast thou heard the saying of St. Ilid, one come from the race of Israel—'There is no madness like extreme anger'." St. Joseph had witnessed the madness that led to the Crucifixion (Iolo MSS., p. 255).

(*f*) THE BARDIC PEDIGREES tracing the descent of King Arthur of Britain maternally from St. Joseph, that of Loth his brother-in-law from Peter, a relative of St. Joseph, and that of the British Princes generally, to Ann " cousin " of the Blessed Virgin Mary and thus confirming the Tradition.[23] It must not be forgotten that St. Joseph was held by Eastern tradition to be " uncle " to the Blessed Virgin Mary.[24] These records of descent are evidence of the deep-felt belief of the connection of Britain and the ancient British Royal Family with St. Joseph, and the Holy Family. Saint Carannog was said to have been descended from the above Anna. So was St. Cadoc. St. David of Wales was said to have been descended from Euguen, son of the sister of the Blessed Virgin Mary. And Beli the Great, the father of King Lud (whence Billingsgate and Ludgate), is stated to have married a consobrina (strictly cousin or niece, but must have been a much earlier kinswoman) of the Blessed Virgin. And nearly every one of these people traced their descent through King Avallach, the grandson of this intermarriage with the Holy Family, surely the King Evelake

[23] Anna, first cousin to the Blessed Virgin Mary, is made daughter to Joseph of Arimathea and ancestress of the British Princes in the Jesus College MS.

[24] He is recorded to be uncle both to the Blessed Virgin and her husband, St. Joseph, in the Holy Family Pedigrees. Harl. MS. (British Museum) 3859, f. 193 b; Jesus College MS. 20; and Appendix 3.

of the Grail stories. These constant assertions, these age-long assertions, are not to be despised.[25]

(10) St. Gregory of Tours, in his *History of the Franks* (p. 133), A.D. 544–595, Haleca, Archbishop of Saragossa, in his *Fragmenta* and the *Chronicon of Pseudo-Dexter*, all unite in saying that Joseph of Arimathea was the first to preach the Gospel in Britain.

Melchior Inchofer, that stout defender of the story of the connection of the Bethany family with Marseilles contends that St. Joseph did accompany them to Marseilles, and cites Isidore, Archbishop of Seville, A.D. 600–636, as to his having been sent to Britain (*De veritate Epistolæ. B. Mariæ ad Messanenses*, cap. 13).

(11) Freculphus, Bishop of Lisieux, A.D. 825–851, at least confirms that St. Philip, who is said to have sent St. Joseph, preached and laboured in France. So that long before William of Malmesbury, the Roman, Eastern, Gallic, and Spanish Churches bore testimony to this fact.

It may not be out of place here to mention that the ancient *Magna Glastoniensis Tabula* which is, and has been for centuries, in the possession of the House of Howard at Naworth Castle, records much already quoted, such as that St. Philip baptized St. Joseph and his son Josephes, and that St. Joseph was appointed by the Blessed Apostle St. John (toiling exclusively for the instruction of the Ephesians) Paranymphos (see pp. 71, 101 and 105) to the Blessed Virgin Mary. And perhaps one might add that Robert Parsons the Jesuit in his *Three Conversions of*

---

[25] *Vide* Professor W. A. S. Hewin's *The Royal Saints of Britain*, pp. 18–20, and *John of Glastonbury*, Hearne's small edition, Vol. 1, pp. 56–57. Rev. Rice Rees, *Welsh Saints*, says that Llyr Llediarth (Lear, father of Bran, grandfather of Caractacus) and Avallach were contemporary with the Christian era, which fits in with the Avallach of the Grail stories (pp. 88–91). See also p. 62 *et seq.*

Britain (St. Joseph, SS. Fagan and Dyfan, and St. Augustine) accepts the story of St. Joseph (including the journey to Marseilles) on the authority of Capgrave, Polydore Vergil, and Camden.

(12) St. POLYCRATES, Bishop of Ephesus (in his Epistle to St. Victor, Pope of Rome, who was martyred under the Emperor Severus, A.D. 193), appears to supply a link. St. Victor was the first to raise the controversy about the keeping of Easter, which lasted till after the Council of Nicæa, A.D. 325. The Eastern Churches kept it on the day of the full moon, whether it fell on a weekday or a Sunday: the Western Churches always on a Sunday. St. Victor was so bitter about it that even in those early days he wished to excommunicate all Churches differing from the Roman custom. There are extant in Eusebius (*Historia Eccles.*, Vol. 24) letters from two eminent ecclesiastics rebuking Pope Victor's policy; one from St. Irenæus (the pupil of St. Polycarp, the disciple of St. John), Bishop of Lyons in the Gallican Church,[26] who with his Church was willing to conform to the Roman and Western usage; the other from the aforesaid St. Polycrates opposing it. In his letter St. Polycrates pleads St. John and St. Philip the Apostle, amongst other illustrious persons, who helped to build up the customs of the Eastern Church. This reference to St. Philip has an interesting bearing on the question of the British Church and its keeping of Easter. If the tradition that St. Philip sent St. Joseph and his companions to Britain from Gaul be true, the British Church might be expected to follow, as it did, St. Philip's method of keeping Easter. The British Church was as insistent upon being Catholic and Apostolic as it was upon being anti-Roman.

[26] Haddan and Stubbs point out (Vol. 1, p. 10) that Lactantius, about A.D. 313, and Sulpicius Severus, about A.D. 400, include the British Church in the Gallican showing the sympathies and affinities of the British Church.

And so after a dispute of 132 years the ultimate decision of the Council of Nicæa, A.D. 325, that Easter was to be kept on a Sunday was binding on it. But it was exactly like the contentious spirit of the race still to differ from Rome in another point of the same question. Accordingly, it was not till the Council of Whitby, A.D. 664, when Saxon Wilfrid persuaded the Council to overthrow the old Celtic discipline, that the British Church agreed to keep Easter on the same Sunday as the Roman and the rest of the Western Church kept it.[27] This bowing to a decision, by keeping Easter on a Sunday, and then keeping up the quarrel by disputing for centuries as to which Sunday to keep it, is very Celtic, and has an analogy in the Welsh adoption of surnames.[28] The Celtic race is the most stubborn in the world, except the Jewish, in spite of their quickness and extraordinary adaptability. The importance of the quotation to our subject is that it seems to give a link between the British Church and St. Philip a thousand years before William of Malmesbury stated it.

(13) Perhaps one may be forgiven for citing here THE

[27] From what Bede wrote, even after the Council of Whitby, the adoption of the Roman Easter was only gradual. The Welsh Church did not adopt it till A.D. 755. Rees's *Essay on Welsh Saints*, p. 65.

[28] When the Welshman Henry VII came to the throne he realized the disadvantages of Welsh nomenclature. A man might have twenty-eight names or more—John, son of David, son of Thomas, son of Llewellyn, etc., being John ap David ap Thomas ap Llewellyn, etc. He therefore decreed that Welsh families were to take surnames. Only the principal families took them at once. They were too illustrious for their disobedience to escape notice. The others adopted a subterfuge, appearing to comply, but clinging to their Celtic tradition. The above pedigree then became John Davis, David Thomas, Thomas Llewellyn. This continued in some cases to quite modern times, and so did the *ap*. Both the ecclesiastical and the civil pieces of conduct are most Celtic.

GREAT SILENCE OF THE ROMAN CHURCH as to St. Joseph's life
and death as in itself equal to a piece of documentary
evidence. St. Joseph was a man of importance, whose
courageous adherence to Christ must have infuriated the
Jews. Yet we hear so little of the fate of this " honourable
counsellor " who defended Our Lord, and claimed and
honoured His dead body when all appeared lost. Britain
was outside the Roman Church, and not altogether within
the Roman Empire. Hence, the silence of the former suggests the truth of the story that he came to Britain. It fits
in.

(14) DATE OF GLASTONBURY'S FEAST OF ST. JOSEPH.
William Goode, the Jesuit, as recorded by Ussher,[29] tells us
that the Feast of St. Joseph was kept at Glastonbury for
six days in the Kalends of August. The Kalends were the
first days of the month. Cressy, the Benedictine, tells us
that St. Joseph died at Glastonbury on July 27, A.D. 82. As
the saint is said to have died on July 27, and his feast was
kept in the early days of August, it looks like an unbroken
record of the date of his burial. The Greek Church
confirms this by keeping the Feast on July 31. In its commemoration it tells that St. Joseph suffered much from the
Jews because he bore witness to the Resurrection, but that
" he died in peace ".

[29] Archbishop Ussher. Cap. 2, and Edward Maihew's *Con-
gregat. Angl. Ordinis Benedict*, Tab. 2, pp. 1118–1119.

CHAPTER 8

THE COMING OF ST. PHILIP TO FRANCE

SEEING how persistent from several sources is the statement that St. Philip sent St. Joseph, his son, and ten other companions from France to convert Britain, it is important to see whether we have any corroborative evidence of St. Philip ever having been in France or Gaul. There is.

(1) ISIDORE, Archbishop of Seville, A.D. 600–636, whom Dr. William Smith (*Dictionary of Christian Biography*) calls "undoubtedly the greatest man of his time in the Church of Spain . . . a voluminous writer of great learning. . . . He had also a trained and cultivated mind" wrote thus: "Philip of the city Bethsaida, whence also came Peter, preached Christ to the Gauls, and brought barbarous and neighbouring nations, seated in darkness and close to the swelling ocean to the light of knowledge and port of faith. Afterwards he was stoned and crucified, and died in Hierapolis, a city of Phrygia, and having been buried with his corpse upright along with his daughters rests there" (*De ortu et obitu Patrum*, Cap. LXXIII, 131).

Archbishop Ussher tells us that the above quotation asserting that St. Philip preached Christ to the Gauls is found in the MS. *Martyrology of Hieronymus* from which Isidore transcribed nearly everything into his book of the Fathers of the New Testament. This may be the great St. Jerome, born about A.D. 346, or quite probably an earlier Hieronymus contemporary of St. Victor of Rome. The latter was martyred in A.D. 193.

(2) CARDINAL BARONIUS. (*Annales*: Tom. 1, Ann. Christi 44, Claudii Imp. 2, Sec. 32) narrates, "Philip the fifth in

order is said to have adorned Upper Asia with the Gospel,[1] and at length at Hierapolis at the age of 87 to have undergone martyrdom, which also John Chrysostom hands down,[2] and they say that the same man travelled over part of Scythia, and for some time preached the Gospel along with Bartholemew.[3] In Isidore one reads that Philip even imbued the Gauls with the Christian faith, which also in the Breviary of Toledo of the School of Isidore is read. But we have said in our notes to the Roman Martyrology that ' to the Galatians ' must be corrected in the place of ' to the Gauls '." But the learned Archbishop Ussher says, " I am not at all satisfied here with the conjecture of Baronius in transferring the statements of Isidore from our Gauls to the Galatians of Asia; much less with the temerity of a recent Editor of the works of Isidore, Jacobus Breulius, in substituting Galatians for the Gauls in the text itself, without any reference to the ancient reading " (*Brit. Ecc. Antiq.*, Cap. II).

(3) JULIAN, Archbishop of Toledo (A.D. 680–690), whom Dr. William Smith (*Dictionary of Christian Biography*) calls " the last eminent Churchman of West Gothic Spain, and next to Isidore of Seville perhaps the most eminent ". Archbishop Ussher tells us (*Antiquities*, Cap. 2) that " he writing on the Prophet Nahum assigned Gaul to Philip ".

(4) BEDE, born about A.D. 673. Archbishop Ussher also tells (*Antiquities*, Cap. 2) that " Bede (or whoever was the author of *Collections and Flowers*) also assigned Gaul to Philip at the foot of the 3rd tome of his works ".

(5) FRECULPHUS, Bishop of Lisieux in France,[4] A.D. 825–

[1] Niceph. 2, Cap. 39. Metaphr, die 15 Novemb.
[2] Chrysostom. No. de 12. Apostl.
[3] I demque supra. Niceph, et Metaphr.
[4] Freculphus's book was in the catalogue of Glastonbury Abbey Library A.D. 1248. William of Malmesbury refers to it. If there in 1129, and doubtless it was, he saw it.

851, wrote (*Tom. posterior Chronicorum*, Lib. II, Cap. IV), "Philipp of the City of Bethsaida whence also came Peter, of whom in the Gospels and Acts of the Apostles praiseworthy mention is often made, whose daughters also were outstanding prophetesses, and of wonderful sanctity and perpetual virginity, as ecclesiastical history narrates, preached Christ to the Gauls." He then proceeds to quote Isidore.

(6) St. Epiphanius, a.d. 315–407, Bishop of Salamis, "one of the most zealous champions of orthodox faith and monastic piety" (Smith's *Dict. of Christ. Biog.*), wrote: "The ministry of the divine word having been entrusted to St. Luke, he exercised it by passing into Dalmatia, into Gaul, into Italy, into Macedonia, but principally into Gaul, so that St. Paul assures him in his epistles about some of his disciples—'Crescens,' said he, ' is in Gaul.' In it must not be read in Galatia as some have falsely thought, but in Gaul." Pere Longueval remarks that this sentiment was so general in the East, that Theodoret who read " in Galatia " did not fail to understand "Gaul" because as a matter of fact the Greeks gave this name to Gaul, and the Galatians had only thus been named because they were a colony of Gauls (*Memoire de l'Apostolat de St. Mansuet* (*vide* p. 83) par l'Abbe Guillaume, p. II).

Perhaps it may be pointed out that Edouard de Bazelaire supports this view of Crescens being in Gaul, and not in Galatia. He traces St. Paul about the year 63 along the Aurelian Way from Rome to Arles in France.[5] He names his three companions: St. Luke, who had just written the Acts; Trophimus whom he left at Arles; Crescens, whom he sent to Vienne. An inscription of this period has been found to the memory of Nero for having purged that province of brigands, and of those who sought to introduce

[5] *Predication du Christianisme dans les Gaules*, Tom. IX, p. 198.

a new superstition (*Les Annales de Philosophic*, Tome LXIV, p. 277). De Bazelaire goes on to say: " On his return he retook Trophimus with him, and was not able to keep him as far as Rome, for he wrote from there to Timothy ' Hasten and come and join me as soon as possible. Crescens is in the Gauls. I have left Trophimus sick at Millet ' [Miletus]." The Abbe Maxime Latour referring to Trophimus being in Gaul says, " In 417 the Pope Zozimus recognized in the Church of Arles the right of being Metropolitan over all the district of Narbonne because Trophimus its first Bishop had been for the Gauls the source of life whence flowed the streams of faith."[6]

All this goes to prove that Gaul was known as Galatia. And their chronicling St. Paul's and his companions' journey does not in the least mean that they deny St. Philip's. For the same M. Edouard de Bazelaire quotes M. Chateaubriand as saying, "Peter sent missionaries into Italy, *in the Gauls*, and on the coast of Africa." The part that St. Peter played is duly emphasized by many illustrious Roman historians. And without St. Peter in the least exercising any primacy, this ardent and potent man might well have influenced his compatriot from Bethsaida.

(7) It is quite important to know that the Churches of Vienne and Mayence in Gaul claim Crescens as their founder. This goes far to corroborate that Galatia in II Timothy iv, 10, means Gaul, and not its colony Galatia in Asia, and that Isidore meant to say that St. Philip preached to the Gauls, and not to the Galatians of Asia.

(8) We have seen that the *Recognitions of Clement* (2nd

[6] *Revue des Sciences Ecclesiastiques*, July 1861. Zozimus, who succeeded Pope Innocent I, only reigned from March 17, 417, till December 25, 418, but he made two important decisions. Besides establishing the precedence of Arles over all French Bishoprics, he finally condemned Pelagius, whom at one time he had been thought to favour.

century) stated that St. Clement of Rome, going to
Caesarea, found St. Joseph of Arimathea there with St.
Peter, Lazarus, the Holy Women and others, a quite likely
place for the start of the voyage of St. Joseph and the
Bethany Family and others to Marseilles. Caesarea was the
home of St. Philip in the Bible story. Afterwards tradition
brings him to France, whence he sent St. Joseph to Britain.
William of Malmesbury, quoting Freculphus, calls Joseph,
St. Philip's "dearest friend". They must have been in
close association. Tradition brings the Holy Women and
St. Joseph to France. All the way up the Rhone Valley, as
we have seen, from Marseilles to Mortaix, we find constant
memories of the occupants of that boat without oars and
sails. From Morlaix in Brittany it is a short step to Cornwall in Britain. The route from Marseilles must have been
known well to St. Joseph. It was that of his fellow traders,
seeking ore. From Cornwall an ancient road led to the
mines of Mendip, remains of which exist. Arviragus's
reception of St. Joseph, though unconverted, suggests a
very possible previous acquaintance. Testimony from the
Early Fathers, and varied branches of the Church, show
that the Church was here in earliest days. This stream of
tradition, supported in so many ways, supplies an answer
as to how it came here.

CHAPTER 9

THE COMING OF ST. SIMON ZELOTES

THERE is Eastern confirmation of the story that St. Simon came here.

(1) DOROTHEUS, Bishop of Tyre (A.D. 303), or the writer who attributed the Synopsis to him, in his *Synopsis de Apostol.* (9. Simon Zelotes) says: " Simon Zelotes preached Christ through all Mauitania, and Afric the less. At length he was crucified at Brittania, slain and buried."

(2) NICEPHORUS, Patriach of Constantinople and Byzantine historian, A.D. 758–829, wrote (Book II, c. 40): " Simon born in Cana of Galilee who for his fervent affection for his Master and great zeal that he showed by all means to the Gospel, was surnamed Zelotes, having received the Holy Ghost from above, travelled through Egypt and Africa, then through Mauretania and all Lybia, preaching the Gospel. And the same doctrine he taught to the Occidental Sea, and the Isles called Britanniæ."

(3) GREEK MENOLOGY. The Menology of the Greek Church celebrates St. Simon's Day on May 10, and supports the statements of his having preached and been martyred in Britain (Baronius, *Annales Ecclesiastici*, under A.D. 44. Sec. XXXVIII).

CHAPTER 10

THE COMING OF ARISTOBULUS

THERE is a very considerable consensus of authority for saying that Aristobulus came to Britain.

(1) HIPPOLYTUS, born about A.D. 160, the most learned member of the Roman Church of that period (who had heard the lectures of St. Irenaeus, born thirty years before him, the pupil of Polycarp the beloved of St. John), who was probably Bishop of the Greeks in Rome during the episcopates of Zephyrinus and Callixtus, in his list mentions Aristobulus as "Bishop of the Britons".

(2) THE MARTYROLOGIES OF THE GREEK CHURCH. The Greek Menology for March 15 says: "Aristobulus was one of the seventy disciples, and a follower of St. Paul the Apostle, along with whom he preached the Gospel to the whole world, and ministered to him. He was chosen by St. Paul to be the missionary bishop to the land of Britain, inhabited by a very warlike and fierce race. By them he was often scourged, and repeatedly dragged as a criminal through their towns, yet he converted many of them to Christianity. He was there martyred after he had built churches and ordained deacons and priests for the island."

(3) HALECA, Bishop of Augusta, says: "The memory of many martyrs is celebrated by the Britons, especially that of St. Aristobulus, one of the seventy disciples" (*Halecae Fragmenta in Martyr*).

(4) ST. DOROTHEUS, Bishop of Tyre, A.D. 303, or whoever wrote the tract attributed to him, says: "Aristobulus, whom Paul saluted, writing to the Romans, was Bishop of Britain" (*Synopsis de Apostol.*, Synops. 23, "Aristobulus").

(5) St. Ado, Archbishop of Vienne (A.D. 800–874), in the *Adonis Martyrologia* for March 17, says: "Natal day of Aristobulus, Bishop of Britain, brother of St. Barnabas the Apostle,[1] by whom he was ordained Bishop. He was sent to Britain, where after preaching the truth of Christ, and forming a Church, he received martyrdom."

(6) Achau Saint Prydain (*Genealogies of the Saints of Britain*): "There came with Bran the Blessed from Rome to Britain—Arwystli Hen [Aristobulus the Aged], Ilid, Cyndaf,[2] man of Israel, Maw or Mawan, son of Cyndaf." Bran and Caractacus were taken prisoners to Rome in A.D. 51. The latter at any rate stayed seven years. Aristobulus is said to have been the father-in-law of St. Peter. This is quite consistent with his being called " the Aged ". In the Triads he is termed " a man of Italy ", in contradiction to his companions. This is interesting in view of St. Paul's reference to his household in Rome (Romans xvi, 10). In the Silurian list he is styled Confessor or Instructor to Bran.

Here, then, is very early Eastern, Roman, Greek and British Church testimony. One of the scenes of the labours of Aristobulus or Arwystli is still called Arwystli in Montgomeryshire on the Severn. It is most interesting to note that Ilid is said to have founded his mission at Cor-Eurgain, at Llan Ilid in Glamorganshire, under the protection of

[1] It is interesting that Beatus (*vide* p. 127) is said to have been baptized in Britain by Barnabas, a companion of Aristobulus.

[2] Cyndaf means Chief or Head. Ilid is believed to be the British name for Joseph of Arimathea, and Mawan is considered to be the latter's son Josephes, from whom King Arthur is said to have been descended on his mother's side. For the British account of the coming of Christianity see *Essay on the Welsh Saints* by the Rev. Rice Rees, London, 1836, and 3rd Series of Welsh Triads—" Myvyrian Archaeology ", Vol. 2, Triads 13 and 35.

Bran, Cyllinus (afterwards St. Cyllinus) his grandson, and Eurgain his grand-daughter (afterwards St. Eurgain) and her husband Salog, from whom Caer Salog or Salisbury took its name. Caractacus returned from Rome later. Cor-Eurgain or Llan Ilid was the other cradle and centre of Christianity in Britain, only a little later in date than Avalon or Glastonbury (*vide* the Rev. R. W. Morgan's *St. Paul in Britain*, pp. 157 and 161).

Aristobulus is said to have died at Glastonbury A.D. 99 (Cressy, a Benedictine monk, 1605–1674). The great abbey at Glastonbury was a Benedictine one, and the Benedictines on the Continent treasured much of its lore, and a few of its relics. But Alford (*Regia Fides*, p. 41) says that Aristobulus was Zebedee, the father of SS. James and John, and the husband of Mary Salome,[3] and that he went to Rome with St. Peter. Thence, leaving his family he was sent to Britain, where he died as a Martyr in the second year of Nero, A.D. 58. Seeing that he was Aristobulus the Aged, this date is much more likely than Cressy's A.D. 99, unless he earned his title " Aged " in this country. It is ridiculous to expect exactness of dates at this distance of time. But may not Mary Salome be muddled with another Salome? Was Aristobulus one of the family of Herods? Aristobulus was a common name in that family. An Aristobulus (a Herod) was uncle of the saintly St. Sabrina. He was the son of another Aristobulus who married Salome, daughter of Philip and Herodias, of dancing fame. And this younger Aristobulus (there were three in the Herod family) was a contemporary and second cousin of King Agrippa and Drusilla who married Felix of the Acts. So the dates

[3] The pedigree of the Holy Family in our College of Arms (Roll 23, Box 26) gives three Maries as half-sisters, viz. the Blessed Virgin Mary, Mary daughter of Cleophas and wife of Alphaeus, and Mary daughter of Salome and wife of Zebedee. (See Appendix 3.)

fit in. (Professor W. A. S. Hewin's *Royal Saints of Britain*, pp. 28 and 29).[4] Cressy says that St. Paul ordained Aristobulus Bishop for Britain. Robert Parsons cites Mirmannus and Baronius as to Aristobulus being a Bishop in Britain.

[4] Professor Hewin (p. 29) thinks Aristobulus, Bishop for Britain, to have been quite possibly son of Herod, King of Chalcis, and great-grandson of Herod the Great. Herod, King of Chalcis, died A.D. 48.

CHAPTER II

THE COMING OF ST. PAUL

(1) ST. CLEMENT OF ROME, A.D. 30–100, wrote: "Paul, also having seven times worn chains, and been hunted and stoned, received the prize of such endurance. For he was the herald of the Gospel to the West, as well as in the East, and enjoyed the illustrious reputation of the faith in teaching the whole world to be righteous. And after he had been *to the extremity of the West* he suffered martyrdom before the sovereigns of mankind; and thus delivered from this world, he went to his holy place, the most brilliant example of steadfastness that we possess" (Epistle to the Corinthians, C.5). St. Clement belonged to the first century, knew St. Paul personally, and was the third Bishop of Rome. St. Paul speaks of him in his Epistle to the Philippians, iv, 3, thus: "With Clement also and other my fellow labourers whose names are in the book of life"; and Irenaeus, born about A.D. 130, himself the pupil of Polycarp the friend of St. John, thus speaks of him: "Clement, who had seen the blessed Apostles and conversed with them; who had the preaching of the Apostles still sounding in his ears, and their traditions before his eyes."[1]

(2) THEODORET THE BLESSED, Bishop of Cyrus near Antioch in Syria, born about A.D. 390, called "facile princeps among his brethren for varied learning" by Dr. Bright,[2] and "an accomplished man of letters . . . a Church historian learned, and generally impartial" by Dr. William

---

[1] The missionary companionship of Mansuetus of Britain with St. Clement of Rome has already been mentioned.

[2] Later treatise of St. Athanasius, Library of Fathers, p. 149.

Smith,[3]; of whom Newman in his *Historic Sketches* wrote:
" He has a place of his own in the literature of the first centuries, and a place in which he has no rival "[4]; and of whom
Bishop Lightfoot wrote: "His commentaries on St. Paul
. . . have been assigned the palm over all patristic exposi-
tions of scripture."[5] Such a man's definite statements cannot lightly be dismissed, and afford early documentary
support to ancient traditions. He, writing about A.D. 435,
said of St. Paul (the leather-worker):

(*a*) " Our fishermen and tax gatherers and the leather-
worker have brought to all men the laws of the Gospel,
and they persuaded not only Romans and their tributaries,
but also the Scythians and Sauromatian nations, and
Indians . . . and Britons, and Cimmerians (or Cimbrians),
and Germans, to accept the laws of the Crucified " (Graec.
aff. cur. Sermo. IX).

(*b*) " St. Paul reached Spain and brought salvation to the
Islands of the sea " (Bishop Edwards of St. Asaph's *Landmarks in the History of the Welsh Church*, p. 4), which fits
in with St. Jerome's statement that, besides visiting Spain,
St. Paul went " from ocean to ocean ", and St. Chrysostum's
that he went " from Illyricum to the very ends of the
earth ".

(3) SOPHRONIUS, Patriarch of Jerusalem, A.D. 633–637,
" the unwearied champion of the orthodox faith against
the monotheistic heresy, not unworthy to be ranked with
Athanasius and Cyril among the defenders of the truth
against successive depravations."[6] Robert Parsons in his
Three Conversions of England (p. 22) cites him as saying
in his sermon on " The Nativity of the Apostles " that St.
Paul came to Britain. He also cites

[3] Smith and Wace's *Dict. Christ. Biog.* under Theodoret.
[4] Vol. III, p. 326.
[5] The Epistle to the Galatians.
[6] Smith and Wace, *Dic. Christ. Biog.*, Vol. IV, p. 719.

(4) VENANTIUS FORTUNATUS, Bishop of Poitiers, born
about A.D. 530, the well-known Christian hymn-writer,
author of *Vexilla Regis* ("The Royal Banners forward go"),
first sung in the great procession when Fortunatus went
out to meet the relic of the Holy Cross which the Emperor
Justin II was sending to the Convent of Poitiers which
Fortunatus's great friend, Queen Radegunda, was founding.
He speaks of St. Paul "crossing the ocean" and visiting
"Britain and the extreme West". It must not be forgotten
that this cultivated literary man must have met many of
the refugee Britons who had fled to France before the
Saxon invader and would have learnt many traditions from
them.

(5) A very ancient tradition assigns the foundation of
Bangor Abbey to St. Paul. Its rule was known as the Rule
of Paul. The Abbots claimed to be his successors. Over
every gate was his command: "If any will not work,
neither shall he eat." Pelagius, A.D. 354–424 (a translation
of Morgan), the heretic who convulsed Christendom, was
the twentieth Abbot. St. Hilary and St. Benedict called it
the Mother of all Monasteries. (The monastery proper at
Glastonbury was not founded till the days of St. Patrick.
The successors of St. Joseph and his companions till then
lived at the foot of the Tor separately as Anchorites.)[7]

---

[7] *Vide* earlier references.

PART IV

EVIDENCES

EARLY MISSIONS FROM BRITAIN
EARLY FATHERS, DIOCLETIAN PERSECUTION, CHURCH
COUNCILS, and PELAGIAN HERESY
CONCLUSION

CHAPTER 12

EARLY MISSIONS FROM BRITAIN

JUST as in the early British days British arms over-ran the Continent, and crossed the Alps before Hannibal did, and sacked Rome under Beli Mawr (the Great) and Bran his brother (Belinus and Brennus), so British Missionaries from the newly planted Church soon showed the virility of their Church by invading Europe.[1]

(1) BEATUS, a noble Briton, whose pre-baptismal name was Suetonius, converted and baptized in Britain (tradition says by St. Barnabas)[2] converted Switzerland. His cell, where he died at a great age, A.D. 96, is still shown at Vnterseen on Lake Thun.[3] Alford says that Bede wrote of him, but does not say in what book, and that he is commemorated in the Roman Martyrology.

(2) MANSUETUS, born in Ireland of noble family, converted and baptized in Britain, said to have been a disciple of St. Peter, was sent in company with St. Clement of Rome, a friend and pupil of the Apostles (afterwards the third Bishop of Rome) to preach the Gospel in France. He founded the Church in Lorraine, and then penetrated to Illyria in the east of Europe, east of the Adriatic, where he was martyred in A.D. 89 or 110.[4]

[1] Those who glibly reject Geoffrey of Monmouth's *History* have to account for the amazing fact that this glorious Celtic record is written by a man half Norman, half Saxon. The hatred between the Celts, Saxons and Normans was prodigious.
[2] St. Barnabas is said to have been a brother of Aristobulus.
[3] *Theat. Magn. Brit.*, Lib., vi., p. 9.
[4] ' Mersæus de Sanctis Germaniæ," *Guilliman Helvet. Hist.*, Lib. 1, Cap. 15. *Hen Pantaleon de Viris illust. Germ.*, Part 1, " L'Apostolat de S. Manouel " by L'Abbé Guillaume, p. 33.

According to Alford in his *Reg. Fid. Brit.* (pp. 28–29) he was consecrated Bishop to the Lotharingians as early as A.D. 49. He also states that he is commemorated in the Gallican Martyrology on September 3. Arnold Mirmannus says that he was baptized in the year A.D. 40.

(3) MARCELLUS, a noble Briton, became third Bishop of Tongres and founded the Archbishopric of Treves, the princely Archbishopric which for centuries dominated the Gallican Church. Almost all the early Archbishops of Treves were Britons. He lived and died, it is stated, as a martyr in A.D. 166.[5]

(4) ST. CADVAL, a British missionary, founded A.D. 170 the Church of Tarentum in Italy, and the Cathedral of Taranto is dedicated to him. (MS. Vellum of the Church of Tarentum. Catalogue of Saints in the Vatican, A.D. 1641, Moronus de Ecclesia Tarentina.)

---

[5] Marsæus, *De Archiepiscopis Treviensium*, and Pantalion, *De Viis Illus. Germaniæ*, Part I.

CHAPTER 13

EARLY FATHERS, DIOCLETIAN PERSECUTION, CHURCH COUNCILS, AND PELAGIAN HERESY

(1) IRENAEUS, *circa* A.D. 125–189. The great Irenaeus, Bishop of Lyons A.D. 177, brought up in the East, pupil of St. Polycarp the pupil of St. John, wrote: "For the Church, though scattered through all the inhabited world as far as the ends of the earth, carefully keeps guard as the occupier of one house . . . and proclaims in harmony the same things . . . as one possessed of one mouth . . . and neither the Churches among the Germans, nor among the Iberians, nor the Kelts, nor those in the East, nor in Egypt, nor in Libya, nor those settled in the midst of the world, have believed differently, nor have differently handed things down." (*Irenaeus against Heresy*, 1, 10 (ed. Paris, 1710).) Professor Lumby felt that it was difficult from the context for the Churches of the Kelts to mean anything except the Churches of France and Britain. I am indebted to the late Mr. F. Bligh Bond, F.R.I.B.A., for drawing my attention to this passage and sending me the original Greek in June 1944, less than a year before his death. (See Appendix 6.)

(2) TERTULLIAN, A.D. 155–222, the Early Father, the first great genius after the Apostles among Christian writers, writing in A.D. 192, said: "The extremities of Spain, the various parts of Gaul, the regions of Britain which have never been penetrated by the Roman Arms [such as Avalon or Glastonbury, and Cor-Eurgain] have received the religion of Christ." (Tertullian, *Def. Fidei*, p. 179.)

(3) ORIGEN, another Early Father (A.D. 185–254), who did
so much to make Christianity a success, whose praise is in
all the Churches, wrote:

(*a*) "The divine goodness of Our Lord and Saviour is
equally diffused among the Britons, the Africans, and
other nations of the world."[1] According to Cressy, the
Benedictine, who through the Benedictine monastery at
Glastonbury was steeped in English traditions, Theanus,
the first Bishop of London, died A.D. 185, the year in which
Origen was born.[2]

(*b*) Homil IV, in Ezek., Hieron interpr. A.D. 239: "For
when did the land of the Britons before the advent of
Christ consent to the religion of one God? . . . But now
because of the Churches, which occupy the bounds of the
world, the whole earth with joy calls to the Lord of Israel."
(III, 370 Delarue.)

(*c*) Homil VI, in Luc. I, 24, Hieron interpr.: "The grace
of our Lord and Saviour is ever with those who are cut

[1] Origen. In Psalm cxlix.
[2] Interesting hanging tablets in the vestry of the ancient
Church of St. Peter, Cornhill, London (quoted by Archbishop
Ussher, in 1639), state that in A.D. 179 Good King Lucius aforesaid founded that church, the first Christian church in London,
which became the archiepiscopal seat of the South. Bishop
Godwin (de Praesulibus, pp. 169–170) says that Theanus,
helped by Cyranus, pincerna to King Lucius, built St. Peter's.
He gives a list of Archbishops of London from Theanus
(d.185) to Theonus (the 16th) who fled into Wales in 586 with
his brothers of York and Caerleon, the year before Augustine
came.

Triad 85, 3rd Series, claims that Lucius also built the first
Church at Llandaff, so Glastonbury (St. Michael's on the Tor),
London, and Llandaff, Britain's most ancient ecclesiastical
centres, all commemorate Lucius or Lleiffer Mawr. The Triad
is supported by the fact that there are four churches near
Llandaff dedicated to SS. Medwy, Elfan, Dyfan, and Fagan,
of Lucian fame.

off from our world in Britain, and with those who are in
Mauretania, and with all under the sun who have believed
in His name. See, therefore, the goodness of the Saviour,
how it is spread over the whole world." (III, 939 Delarue.)

(4) EUSEBIUS writing *circa* A.D. 315 (see p. 85).

(5) MELLO, of Britain, stated by Petits Bollandistes of
Guerin to have been born at Cardiff, was consecrated first
Bishop of Rouen in France A.D. 256.[3] He apparently died
about October 22, 280. There is a church of St. Mellor near
Cardiff.

(6) In the DIOCLETIAN PERSECUTION,[4] A.D. 303, there were
martyred in Britain Stephen and Argulius, both Bishops
of London; Socrates, Bishop of York; Amphibalus, Bishop
of Llandaff; Nicholas, Bishop of Penrhyn (Glasgow);
Melior, Bishop of Carlisle; St. Alban[5]; Julius and Aaron,
priests at Caerleon; and over 889 communicants in different
grades of society (*Martyrology of Nother*, A.D. 894;
Haddan and Stubbs, Vol. 1, p. 32; Gildas, A.D. 516–570, *De
Excidio Brittaniæ*, Hist. VIII, Section 10, 10). The terrors
of this persecution in Britain were recorded by friend and
foe. Constantius, of Lyons, who wrote the life of Germanus
about A.D. 500, and Venantius Fortunatus, Bishop of
Poitiers, A.D. 530–609, both of the friendly Gallican Church,
and the Venerable Bede, of the hostile Saxon one (A.D.
673–735), alike tell the story of St. Alban, Amphibalus,
Aaron and Julius.

The remains of a chapel dedicated to St. Aaron still

---

[3] Haddan and Stubbs, Vol. 1, pp. 4 and 33. Capgrave, *Nov.
Leg. Angl.*, p. 229 *et seq.* Smith's and Wace's *Dictionary of
Christian Biography*, iii, p. 901.

[4] Bede, Caps. 6–8.

[5] Dr. Wm. Smith, and Wace, say of St. Alban, " It is at least
certain that 125 years after the latest date assigned to Alban's
martyrdom, 144 years after the earliest, i.e. A.D. 429, Germanus
visited his relics in Britain." *Dic. Christian Biog.* I, p. 69. (Constantius Vit. Herman I, 25.) Haddan and Stubbs, I, 15.

stand, incorporated with a cow-shed at Penafor Farm near
Caerleon. A chapel of St. Julian was attached to St. Julian
Manor-house in that neighbourhood (once occupied by
Lord Herbert of Cherbury, but pulled down by one of the
Fairbanks family to enlarge his kitchen!). A few pieces of
it are in the parish church of Newport, Monmouth. A
neighbouring chapel to St. Alban disappeared long ago.
It is of extreme interest that these three chapels dedicated
to three martyrs of the Diocletian Persecution were in a
group close to Caerleon. Aaron and Julian were priests
there. Amphibalus was a monk there and went on a
journey to Rome with Alban, who was going to serve there
as a soldier for seven years. Amphibalus converted him.
Alban returned to his native Verulam (or St. Albans). Both
were martyred. Some think that Amphibalus was the
priest whom Alban died to save.

The persecution is also recorded by Sozomen about A.D.
436, *Hist. Eccl.* I, 6 (Haddan and Stubbs I, 4), and even
earlier by Lactantius (A.D. 260–340) about A.D. 313, *De Mort.
Persecut*, XV, XVI.

(7) EBORIUS of York, RESTITUTUS of London, and
ADELFIUS of Caerleon, British Bishops, as were also
Sacerdos, a priest, and Arminius, a deacon, were present at
the Church Council of Arles A.D. 314[6]; and British Bishops

---

[6] By a curious slip the writer of the ancient MS. describes
Adelfius as "de civitate Colonia Londinensium", having
evidently got the word Londinensium into his head from the
line above. It is surmised that he meant to write Legionum,
"the City of Legions", being the ancient name of Caerleon
Vawe, or Chester. On the other hand, the three ancient archbishoprics were London, York, and Caerleon-on-Usk (*vide*
Mansi, Vol. II, pp. 476–7). The Bishoprics of London, York
and Caerleon were not called Archbishoprics, nor indeed were
there any Archbishoprics until after the Council of Nicaea,
A.D. 325. Geoffrey of Monmouth distinctly says (Bk. 4, cap.
XIX) that the Archflamens (Archdruids) of London, York, and

were also present at Nicaea A.D. 325,[7] Sardica in Illyria A.D. 347, and Ariminium, Italy, A.D. 359. Arles was the first Council called by the first Christian Emperor, Constantine, Nicaea was the first Oecumenical Council called by him, and it is interesting to note that hardly ten of the 318 bishops present were of the Latin-speaking Church. It is interesting to note that the British bishops, alone of bishops, in proud independence refused the journey allowance and maintenance offered to them at the Council of Arles.[8]

Three British bishops were too poor to travel to the Council of Ariminium A.D. 350 at their own expense.

(8) HILARY, Bishop of Poitiers (A.D. 300–367), the celebrated bishop and theologian, the active and ardent opponent of the Arians and supporter of St. Athanasius, congratulates the Britons on their freedom from heresy in A.D. 358 (*vide* Ussher, *de Brit. Eccl. Primord.*, Cap. VIII,[9] and Haddan and Stubbs I, 9).

(9) THE EMPEROR CONSTANTINE THE GREAT. *Epist. ad. Eccles. ap. Euseb. Vit. Const.*, III, XIX, A.D. 325, says that bishops from the City of the Romans, and Africa, all Italy,

---

the City of Legions, became Archbishops in King Lucius' reign, and that the City of Legions was situated on the River Uske in Glamorganshire. The Rev. Rice Rees in his *Welsh Saints* says that the names of those three bishops are not recorded in Welsh documents, but he points out that the name Adelfius is practically that of Cadfrawl, a Welsh bishop. Both mean " Brother ". Eborius, and Restitutus would be Enfrog and Rhystyd, names common in Wales later. Haddan and Stubbs, Vol. I, p. 7, point out that York being put as the first province is a special mark of the reign of Constantine.

[7] Where they must have met Eusebius.

[8] *Aug. Opp.*, IX App. 1095 A; Haddan and Stubbs, I, 7; Mansi *Concilia* II, 466, 467; Godwin de Proesutibus, 1743, p. 170, etc.

[9] He wrote to " Bishops of the provinces of Britain ".

Egypt, Spain, Gaul, and Britain . . . agreed at the Council of Nicaea to the keeping of Easter on one day.

(10) VICTRICIUS, Bishop of Rouen, another Gallican bishop, and a friend of St. Martin of Tours (said to be maternal uncle of St. Patrick) says that he came at the request of his fellow bishops in Britain to compose British controversies in the year A.D. 394 or 395.[10]

(11) ST. ATHANASIUS, A.D. 353. (*a*) Describes the Churches of Britain as adhereing to the faith of the Council of Nicaea (A.D. 325) (*vide* Ussher *De Brit. Eccl. Primord.*, Cap. VIII).

(*b*) Writing about A.D. 350 (*Apol. cont. Arian.*), claims that British bishops joined with more than 300 bishops at the Council of Sardica, A.D. 347, in supporting him against Arianism. (N.B.—They may not all have been present. Some sent their agreement. Restitutus was present.)

(*c*) Writing A.D. 363 (*Synod Epist.* of Church of Alexandria), the Emperor Jovian says that at the Council of Nicaea A.D. 325, the Bishops of Spain and Britain and Gaul and from the East agreed to condemn Arianism.

(12) At the time of the PELAGIAN HERESY there were under Pelagius (b. A.D. 354) in Bangor Abbey alone no less than 2,100 monks (*Vita Pelagii*, p. 3).[11] And the independence of the Church was equal to its numbers. " The British Church is the sole judge in Britain " is Pelagius's dictum, speaking of ecclesiastical matters.

(13) ST. CHRYSOSTOM, Patriarch of Constantinople, A.D. 347–407, writes:

(*a*) *Epist. contra Judæos.* " The British Isles, which are

---

[10] Bishop Edwards of St. Asaph's *Landmarks*, p. 8, and Wace and Smith's *Dic. Christ. Biog.*, Vol. IV, p. 1140.

[11] Bede, Bk. 2, cap. 2, tells us of the same number of monks at Bangor, and records that no less than 1,200 were destroyed by King Ethelfrid (about A.D: 603).

beyond the sea, and which lie in the ocean, have received the power of the Word. Churches are there founded, and altars erected."

(b) *Sermo de utilit. lect. Script.* "Though thou shouldest go to the ocean, to the British Isles, *there thou shouldest hear all men everywhere discoursing matters out of the scriptures*, with another voice indeed, but not another faith: with a different tongue, but the same judgment."

(c) In Epist. ad Cor. XII, Homil 28. "Whenever you come to a Church, even in the Spains, or Persia, or even in the very British Isles, you hear John crying, 'It is not lawful for thee to have thy brother Philip's wife.'"

(d) In Matth. Homil 80. "And the memory of what happened did not fade. But both Persians, and Indians, and Scythians, and Thracians, and Sauromatians, and the race of the Moors, and they who inhabit the British Isles circulate what happened secretly in the house in Judaea concerning the adulterous woman."

(e) Sermon I, in Pentecost: "... and whenever you come to the Indians, the Moors, the Britons, to the inhabited world, you will find 'In the beginning was the Word' and His virtuous life."

(f) An old Latin Translation. "Before this moreover as often as they fed on human flesh in Britain, now they refresh their souls with fasts.[12]

(14) ST. JEROME (a) writing A.D. 378: "From India to Britain all nations resound with the death and resurrection of Christ" (Epist. XIII to Paulinus).

(b) "The Briton, who lives apart from our world, if he go on a Pilgrimage, will leave the western parts and seek

---

[12] These last four quotations are given by Haddan and Stubbs, Vol. I, pp. 10–11.

Jerusalem,[13] known to him by fame only, and by the Scriptures " (Epistle XLIV and Haddan and Stubbs I, II).

(c) " Nor is it to be thought one Church of the City of Rome, another of the whole world. Both the Gauls and Britons, and Africa, and Persia, and the East, and India, and all barbarous nations adore one Christ, obey one rule of faith " (Epist. CI ad Evangel., circa A.D. 398).

(d) " If Christ has not a Church only, or if He has it only in Sardinia, He is made too poor. And if Satan possess the Britons, the Gauls, the East, the peoples of the Indies, the barbarous nations, and almost the whole world, how have the victories of the Cross been carried to the corner of the world? "

(e) Epistle ad Paulinum. " But those who say ' The Temple of God, the Temple of God,' let them hear the Apostle—' Ye are the Temple of God and the Holy Spirit lives in you.' And from Jerusalem and Britain equally the heavenly home lies open. So the Kingdom of God is within you."

(f) Epistle ad Heliodorum. " Add this that before the resurrection of Christ, God was only known in Judea. . . . Where then were the men of the whole world from India to Britain? They were counted by the law of fishes and locusts, and as flies and gnats. Now both the voices and writings of all nations hail the resurrection of Christ."

(g) Epistle 84, ad Oceanum. " The whole world alike has heard from Xenodochium[14] situated in the Port of Rome.

---

[13] Just as St. David did in the 6th century when the Patriarch of Jerusalem gave him the Sapphire Altar of Glastonbury (see the author's *Glastonbury, The Mother of Saints*). Jerusalem, not Rome, was the cynosure of the British Church. Dean Parry of St. David's, in an article in the *Sunday Times*, March 7, 1948, on St. David's Cathedral, mentions a tradition that St. David was consecrated Bishop by John III, Patriarch of Jerusalem.

[14] Founded by Christian Charity. Haddan and Stubbs, I, II.

In one summer Britain has learnt what Egypt and Parthia had known."

(15) ST. AUGUSTINE OF HIPPO (A.D. 354) writing A.D. 408: " How many churches are there not erected in the British Isles which lie in the ocean!" (*Opera. Fol.*, Paris edition, p. 676.)

(16) PRUDENTIUS, born A.D. 348: " . . . the chief Christian poet of early times ",[15] whose works were a mine of information, writing about A.D. 405, tells us that St. Cyprian, the great African saint, by his writings " enthuses the Gauls, and imbues the Britains " (*Peri Stephanon*, XIII, 103).

(17) PALLADIUS, Bishop of Helenopolis, born about A.D. 367, who was ordained by St. Chrysostom, and wrote his *Historia Lauriaca* between A.D. 412 and 420, tells of the coming of Persian and British pilgrims to Syria and Jerusalem before 410. He travelled much in Mesopotamia and Syria and the East generally, and wrote of what he saw. (I. *Hist. Lauriaca*, 118.)

(18) THEODORET (born about A.D. 390) tells of many dwellers in the furthest West, both Spaniards and Britons and Gauls coming to visit St. Simon Stylites at Telanisous near Antioch (Philoth. XXVI, speaking probably of A.D. 423). It is interesting that Dr. W. Smith and Dr. Wace, in the *Dictionary of Christian Biography*, say of St. Simon Stylites that " he was the first of a succession of pillar saints somewhat like the enclosed anchorites of the early Celtic Church except that the latter were enclosed in a cell at the level of the earth; the former were enclosed in a box or a paling at a height varying from 10 to 60 ft. In fact Simeon was himself according to Theodoret originally an enclosed anchorite, and only raised his cell to avoid the honours paid to him." How many and constant are the likenesses between the Eastern and Celtic Churches.

[15] Dr. William Smith's and Professor Wace's *Dict. of Christ. Biog.*, IV, p. 500.

(19) SOZOMEN, the well-known Church historian, born about A.D. 400 in Palestine:

(*a*) In his *Church History* (I, 6) tells of British Christians in the Court of Constantius,[16] the father of Constantine the Great, nearly 200 years before he wrote.[17] He is described as "habitually trustworthy, a conscientious and serious writer.[18]

(*b*) Writing *circa* A.D. 443 (*Hist. Eccl.* VII, 13): "And in this year [A.D. 387] Maximus [of Britain] collected a huge army of British men, and of the neighbouring Gauls (Galaton) and Kelts, and of nations of this sort, and went into Italy, pleading as an excuse that *he would not endure some innovation concerning the faith of his fathers, and ecclesiastical order*, but really grasping for himself the glory of a tyrant".[19] This is an extremely important passage, as showing strong British dislike of, and action against some departure in Rome from the ancient Catholic

---

[16] Constantius is said to have founded from Britain the Colony of Armorica or Brittany in A.D. 284. Later the Emperor Maximus appointed Meriadoc "Duke of the Armorican frontier". In 409 the Roman Magistrates were thrust out, and Conan, who died 921, became King. (Haddan and Stubbs, Vol. 2.)

[17] Constantine's mother was the Empress Helena, the British Princess who was almost certainly the daughter of King Coel, who was buried at Glastonbury. King Coel is said to have been one of the two kings who added to the Hides given by Arviragus to St. Joseph, making them the celebrated Twelve Hides. The Fable that Helena was only a concubine is for ever given the lie by coins where she is called Flavia Helena Augusta, as also by almost contemporary writings. She became by marriage a member of the Flavian Gens, and as the wife of Augustus became Augusta. Indeed she is said by Sulphicus Severus to have reigned as empress with her son.

[18] Dr. William Smith's and Professor Wace's *Dictionary of Christian Biography*, IV, p. 723.

[19] Haddan and Stubbs, Vol. I, p. 12.

faith and order. Having cited earlier an old Breton tradition about Cornwall and the Holy Family, it may not be
out of place here to give a few salient dates of the con-
nection between Britain and Brittany gathered from
Haddan and Stubbs, Vol. 2, pp. 71–74. After raiding Italy
a colony of the above British Emperor Maximus's soldiers
settled in Armorica, or Brittany, in A.D. 387. In 409–512
Roman officers were expelled, and an independent
Armorican state set up under a "King of the Britons".
In A.D. 450 great immigration of Britons; A.D. 470 Riothanus
Rex Britonum helps the Romans against the Goths. From
A.D. 493 to 497 Armoricans were independent allies of
Germans and Franks who had failed to conquer them. In
A.D. 502 Brittany was practically independent, but under
suzerainty of Franks. Rulers no longer were kings, but
earls or dukes. Again in A.D. 512 a further immigration of
Britons took place under King Riwallus or Howel, with a
multitude of ships from oversea. *Bishoprics were founded
for them by Childebert* at Leon, and perhaps at Dol, irre-
spectively of the Archbishopric of Tours. From A.D. 541
to 590 there were differences about Easter. In 561–566
further immigrations of Britons in connection with SS.
Maclovius and Maglovius occurred. From 612 to 632
Cadwallader of Wales took refuge with Duke Solomon,
and again in 664–689 with Duke Alan. We must also
remember that Gildas the Wise founded his British monastery at Ruys in Brittany in 520 (or 540?).[20] These are just
a few dates and events. They were one race and one royal
house with the same traditions.[21] *Vide* Appendix 11.

(c) Sozomen was one of the three great historians who

---

[20] Haddan and Stubbs, Vol. II, p. 74, and V, pp. 40–41.
[21] See also the very early testimony of St. Gildas, *De excidio
Britannico*, also of Nennius and later of Geoffrey of Monmouth, Layaman's *Bruit*, the Trials, the Brut, Gruffydd ap
Arthur, and the *Mabinogion*.

wrote about the Council of Nicaea in A.D. 325. Eusebius, contemporary with and actually prominent at the Council, was the first Socrates, a native and inhabitant of Constantinople, a just and impartial Christian layman, was the second. Sozomen, who came of the third generation of a Christian family, was the third. His history was republished in Bohn's Ecclesiastical Library.

(20) GERMANUS OF AUXERRE and LUPUS OF TROYES were of course the celebrated bishops sent by the Synod of the Gallican Church in A.D. 429 to help the British Church against Pelagianism on the appeal of British bishops, the Celtic Church constantly appealing to the Celtic Church.

(21) VENANTIUS FORTUNATUS spoke of the love of the Britains for St. Martin of Tours who died about A.D. 397 (Poem X, 8). St. Martin was probably the maternal uncle of St. Patrick the great British missionary to Ireland.

(22) ST. PATRICK of Ireland, A.D. 395–472, tells us in his *Confessions* that he was born in Britain, the son of Calpurnius, a deacon, and the grandson of Potitus, a priest. He was buried at Glastonbury.

This ancient claim of Glastonbury's is supported by Fiacc's Hymn. This must have been written in the form in which it has come down to us after A.D. 566 for it mentions the desertion of Tara. Fiacc was a contemporary of St. Patrick. Dr. Loof argues that the hymn was written later, and with the aid of the Memoir of Muirchu, whose father Cogitotus died in 670.[22] Neither the hymn nor the memoir mention Pope Celestine's Commission. The hymn associates St. Patrick with St. Germanus. The *Scholiast* (11th century) commenting on Fiacc's Hymn says "Some say that in Rossdale in the region of Maghloca old Patrick's remains used to be, but it is more correct to say [that they

---

[22] Wace's and Smith's *Dict. of Christian Biog.*, Vol. I, p. 592, and Stokes' *Ireland and the Celtic Church*, p. 29.

were] in Glastonbury of the Gael, a town in the south of England."[23] Professor Stokes[24] quotes thus: "Old Patrick that is in Glaestingaburh [Glastonbury] of the Gael in England, Old Patrick of Ros Dela in Mag Locha, but it is truer that he is in Glastonbury of the Gael in the South of England. For Irishmen used to dwell there in pilgrimage. But his relics are in Old Patrick's tomb in Armagh." This was taken by Professor Stokes from Lebar Brace, p. 94. Thus Glastonbury's claim is much more substantiated than Ireland's claim that the saint was buried in three places—Armagh, Downpatrick, and Saul.

(23) OROSIUS, writing about A.D. 417 (Hist. VII, 40), tells us that Constans, the son of Constantine the Briton who usurped the Imperial Throne of Rome in A.D. 407, had been a monk.[25]

(24) SOCRATES, writing about A.D. 440 (*Hist. Eccl.*, VII, 12), said "Chryanthus was brought down to the Bishop[26] in A.D. 407 . . . having been appointed Vicar of the British Isles."

(25) CONSTANTIUS, of Lyons, the heroic friend of Sidonius Apollinaris, whose courage and enthusiasm in advanced years saved the city of Clermont in Auvergne from Euric the Goth, A.D. 473–492 in his life of St. Germanus (I, 25) tells how the latter brought relics of all the apostles and many martyrs to place in the tomb of St. Alban.

[23] Baring Gould's *Lives of Welsh Saints*, Vol. 2, and Professor Stokes' *Tripartite Life*, Vol. II, p. 247.
[24] *Tripartite Life*, Master of the Rolls Service, p. 505.
[25] Haddan and Stubbs, Vol. III.
[26] Of the Novatians in Constantinople. Haddan and Stubbs, Vol. III.

CHAPTER 14

CONCLUSION

THE foregoing quotations show that there was a great Celtic
Church here, before the heathen Saxons nearly destroyed
her and drove her into the mountains of the west. She was
intimately connected with another great Celtic Church, the
Gallican, and with the Church at Jerusalem. We know
from his letter to St. Gregory that St. Augustine found here
the Gallican custom of Mass, and not the Roman. The
Gallican Church was Eastern in its origin. Pothinus, the
first Bishop of Lyons, came direct from Asia Minor, along
with his successor, the celebrated Irenaeus, who as a child
heard Polycarp the familiar friend of St. John the Divine,
and other disciples of our Lord, as Polycarp stated in his
letter to Florinus. And it was to the Churches of Asia, and
not to Rome, that the Churches of Lyons and Vienne sent
a full account of their terrible martyrdom during the
Aurelian persecution in A.D. 177. Some of the Eastern
marks of the Gallican Church were: (1) veiling of women
on receiving the Eucharist; (2) episcopal blessing preceding
the communion of the people; (3) the blessing of a loaf at
the end of the liturgy. In the controversy about Easter
at the Council of Whitby, Abbot Colman urged that the
British usage could be traced back to St. John.[1] The British
bishops refused to give up their customs at the demand of
St. Augustine without the consent of their people. We are
the sister and not the daughter of Rome! We may add
that the British Church used the old Latin version of the

---

[1] *Vide* Bishop Edwards of St. Asaph, *Landmarks*, p. 10.

Scriptures, which was African in origin, and dated from the 2nd century. In Britain there was a special British version of this old Latin version, made by good British scholars before the 5th century, when the vulgate of St. Jerome began to displace it. Men discussed the Scriptures in their own tongue.[2] The Church was national but progressive, and Catholic. The British Ordinal had special lessons from the British version and special customs of anointing the hands of deacons, and the heads and hands of priests.

Such then, was our Church in those days. Here is a little picture of its vigour. Such then, is the evidence that it is of apostolic origin, independent of and equal with any branch of the Church Catholic. And here in Glastonbury was its cradle. We can still stand and see a church—alas, ruined—on the site of the wattle church built by St. Joseph of Arimathea. From here the Light went forth, from here it soon mingled with kindred Light brought very speedily to our shores. From here in one broad blaze it spread over the British Isles. From here it illumined Ireland, Scotland, Switzerland, parts of France, Spain, Italy, and Eastern Europe. Here almost alone in Britain, the Light and the Perpetual Choir have never ceased. An ancient British Triad speaks of the Three Perpetual Choirs of Britain—Glastonbury, Ambresbury, and Llan Iltud Vawr. Ambresbury fell in the middle of the 6th century. The Romans probably never fully got sway here; certainly not till many were Christians. The Saxons were converted before they reached here. Glastonbury remained British territory till between 652 and 658.[3] The Danes, the ravagers, never got here till the days of Canute, and he granted another charter, and laid a pall of embroidery and

---

[2] St. Chrysostom, *Orat. and O. Theos. Christos.*
[3] Haddan and Stubbs, Vol. III, p. 164. Ina handed it over to Rome about 725.

peacocks' feathers on his rival King Edmund's tomb. All down the ages of warring heathendom the place was almost miraculously preserved. No wonder men called it " The Secret of the Lord ". No wonder that here, from a ravaged country, for centuries men brought their treasured holy things for protection. No wonder that an oath by " The Old Church ", or " Vetusta Ecclesia ", was the most sacred oath that men of this province could take.

Before we close we will quote again, but this time in full, the words of William of Malmesbury, *Acts of the Kings*, Book I, Cap. 2 : " The Church of which we are speaking— from its antiquity called by the Angles by way of distinction ' Ealde Churche ' that is ' The Old Church ' of wattle work at first, savoured somewhat of heavenly sanctity even from its very foundation, and exhaled it over the whole country; claiming superior reverence though the structure was mean. Hence, here arrived whole tribes of the lower orders, thronging every path; here assembled the opulent of their their pomp; and it became the crowded residence of the religious and the literary. . . . This church, then, is certainly the oldest that I am acquainted with in England, and from this circumstance derives its name. In it are preserved the mortal remains of many saints, some of whom we shall notice in our progress, nor is there any corner of the church destitute of the ashes of the holy. The very floor, inlaid with polished stone, and the sides of the altar, and even the altar itself above and beneath, are laden with the multitude of relics. . . . The antiquity and multitude of its saints have endued the place with so much sanctity that, at night, scarcely any one presumes to keep vigil there, or during the day to spit upon its floor: he who is conscious of pollution shudders through his whole frame. No one ever brought hawk or horses within the confines of the neighbouring cemetery who did not depart injured either in them or in himself. . . . It is sufficiently evident that the men of that province had no oath more frequent or more sacred than to swear by The Old Church, fearing the swiftest vengeance on their perjury in this respect. . . . In the meantime it is clear that the repository of so many saints may be deservedly called a heavenly sanctuary on earth. There are numbers of documents, though I abstain from mentioning them[4] for fear of causing weariness, to prove how extremely venerable this place was held by the chief persons of the country, who there more especially chose to await the day of resurrection under the protection of the Mother of God."

To sum up—there is the Glastonbury tradition that St. Joseph brought Christianity here, being sent by St. Philip from France. It is as easy as it is ignorant to scoff at it and say "Where is the proof—nothing before 1129?" (Untrue, as we have seen.) The more cultured way is to say "Can we find any evidence to support the likelihood of this very interesting tradition? St. Clement of Rome, in the 1st century, says that St. Paul went to the extremities of the West. The Early Fathers, Tertullian and Origen, born in the 2nd century, definitely say that Britain had received the Faith in their times. A great historian, Eusebius, born in the 3rd century, distinctly says that the Apostles came to Britain. Hilary, Bishop of Poitiers, born A.D. 300, congratulated the British on their freedom from heresy. Gildas the Wise (born in the early 5th century and an inmate of Glastonbury Abbey) records that Britain received the Faith in A.D. 37, the last year of Tiberius Caesar. We find the Church established here as a Missionary Church as early as the 1st century. Beatus, a Briton, converted Switzerland, and died in A.D. 96. Another Mansuetus, an Irishman, converted and baptized in Britain, a companion of St. Clement of Rome, founded

[4] Alas, that he did not!

the Church of Loraine and Illyria, in the 1st century. Marcellus, a Briton, martyred in 166, founded the Archbishopric of Treves, and St. Cadval, another, founded the Church of Tarentum in Italy in A.D. 170, and the Cathedral of Taranto is dedicated to him. The Church of Britain lost six bishops, and 889 communicants, in the Diocletian Persecution in A.D. 303. The Bishops of London, York, and Caerleon were at the Church Council of Arles in A.D. 315. So the Church was here during 'the first three centuries, and was active. Why should the Arimathean tradition be a fable? It is for those who doubt it to prove that it is an impossible story. They cannot.

We have seen that St. Clement of Rome found St. Joseph of Arimathea, St. Peter, and the Bethany family, at Caesarea, a port on the Mediterranean, very probably the port from which St. Joseph and the Bethany family, sent adrift in the boat, were finally to land at Marseilles. William of Malmesbury tells us that St. Philip sent St. Joseph and his companions from France, finally to arrive at Glastonbury. The learned Isidore, Archbishop of Seville, born A.D. 600, tells us that St. Philip evangelized France and converted neighbouring nations. The 10th-century *Fastes Episcoporum* tell the Aquitaine tradition that St. Martial and his father and mother, Marcellus and Elizabeth, St. Zaccheaus, and St. Joseph of Arimathea, arrived at Limoges in the 1st century, but that St. Joseph did not remain.

Freculphus, French Bishop of Lisieux, born about 800, confirms St. Philip's evangelizing France, and sending St. Joseph and his companions to Britain. It is interesting that a copy of Freculphus's book was in Glastonbury Library, and must have been seen by William of Malmesbury, resident and writing there. We can trace St. Joseph, sent by Jewish persecution from Palestine, with his companions of the boat at Marseilles, evangelizing there, and founding

primitive Bishoprics all along the Rhone Valley, the old
traders' route to Britain, and leaving holy sites which exist
till this day. Leaving his fellow saints to continue their
work in France, he follows the traders' route, so familiar to
him, to Morlaix in Brittany, and with his eleven companions goes to convert his old haunts in Britain, just as
later St. Patrick went successfully to convert the Irish
whom he had learnt to understand during his captivity.
Thus God works. And how striking it is, that when in the
5th century the Pelagian heresy started in Britain it was
Germanus, Bishop of Auxerre in France, and another
French bishop, Lupus Bishop of Troye, who came over to
help purify their sister Church. And it was the great St.
Martin of Tours who was maternal uncle to our St. Patrick.
How unbroken the link between the two Churches! Arch-
bishop Ussher tells us that the fact that St. Philip evange-
lized France is found in *Hieronymus Martyrology* from
which St. Isidore copies so much. This may be the great
St. Jerome born in A.D. 346, or an earlier one mentioned
A.D. 193.

Nor can we forget that the great Greek Church to this
day commemorates Our Lord's disciple St. Simon Zelotes
as having been martyred in Britain and Aristobulus
(named by St. Paul) as having been Bishop in Britain and
martyred here; and that Hippolytus, born about 160, also
records Aristobulus (named in Welsh traditions) as Bishop
of the British. And Dorotheus, Bishop of Tyre (303), tells
of the mission and martyrdom here of St. Simon Zelotes,
as does Nicephorus, Patriarch of Constantinople, born
758.

Again, what links of evidence. How much harder to
reject than to accept with awe and thankfulness the beautiful Arimathean tradition!

APPENDICES

1. Account of St. Joseph's Tomb

2. Kinships of the Holy Family

3. A few salient dates of Glastonbury Abbey, and its Historians

4. Our Lord's Traditional Visit to Britain

5. The late Mr. Frederick Bligh Bond and the Arimathean Tradition

6. Joseph was in the Tin Trade

7. Was the Blessed Virgin Mary buried in St. Mary's, the old wattle church?

8. The close connection between Brittany and Britain

9. Archbishop Ussher's account of the Glastonbury Traditions

10. William of Malmesbury

11. The Glastonbury Tradition and the Precedence of English Ambassadors

12. The Celtic Church

ACCOUNT OF ST. JOSEPH'S TOMB

THE body of St. Joseph, whose burial at the wattle Church of St. Mary was recorded by Maelgwyn of Avalon, writing about A.D. 540[1] lay undisturbed till the year 1345, when Edward III gave his licence to John Bloom of London to dig for the body if the Abbot and Monks permitted. And just as the discovery of the bones of King Arthur at Glastonbury in 1190 were recorded in far-away Essex by the monk Ralph de Coggeshall, so in a far-away Lincolnshire monastery in 1367 we find a monk, R. de Boston, recording that " The bodies of Joseph of Arimathea and his companions were found in Glastonbury ". The remains of St. Joseph were put in a silver casket which could be raised at will from a stone sarcophagus, the base of a shrine to which frequent pilgrimage was made. To go " to Joseph ab Aramathee " was to go on pilgrimage to Glastonbury. One of the early printed books was *De Sancto Joseph ab Armathia*, printed by Richard Pynson, A.D. 1516. He narrates various miracles alleged to have been performed in the year 1502 before the shrine, including the healing of Mrs. Lyte of Lytes Carey, a notable of the neighbourhood, and the Vicar of Wells. This shrine of St. Joseph was at the east end of the crypt under St. Mary's Chapel, and caused the whole chapel constantly to be called St. Joseph's Chapel. Apparently a Norman underground chapel was converted into his shrine. Can this have been the site before the fire of 1184 of the wonderful underground chapel which William of Malmesbury (cap. XL) tells us

[1] *Vide* pp. 13 and 161.

that King Ina caused to be built (about A.D. 700) " below the
Greater Church ", a chapel laden with silver and° gold?
The chapel was originally approached by a stair-case past
the ancient Norman well of St. Joseph, close to where he
was at first buried. Later, in the 15th century, a piece of
great vandalism was carried out. The crypt to the west of
it was dug out, disturbing saintly dead, and raising the
floor of the whole chapel. Thus the increasing flood of
pilgrims were able to approach that way also. The shrine
stood in front of a pillar in the middle of this sanctuary
of the crypt. And overhead, all round this spot, and nowhere else, can be seen the holes in the vaulting where were
fastened the chains from which lights descended. There is
also still to be seen the pedestal on which stood a figure
of St. Joseph to the north of the shrine. This stone altar
tomb, the base of the shrine, like the Holy Thorn, survived the Reformation. Holinshed in his *Chronicle*, A.D.
1577, speaks of St. Joseph's sepulchre as being still in
Glastonbury (Vol. I. p. 40, 1807 ed.) and the learned John
Ray in his *Itinerary* records that on June 22, 1662, " we saw
Joseph of Arimathea's tomb and chapel at the end of the
Church ". As we have seen, the Holy Thorn was cut down
in the Great Rebellion. The aftermath of the same period
saw the altar tomb of St. Joseph leave its shrine. During
the Commonwealth a Nonconformist Divine was put in as
incumbent of the parish church.[2] This was hated by good
Church people. He brought with him some followers. A
whole generation were brought up in theology never heard
before in the Church of England. There were two

[2] I owe the knowledge of John Ray's visit, and *Itinerary*, to
Mr. James Webb, of Redcliffe Buildings, Bristol, who caused
to be put into my hands a little book called *St. Joseph's Chapel,
Glastonbury Abbey*, written by William Mellor, an antiquary
of Derby, in 1873, pleading for its restoration. William Mellor
came here and talked to high and low, and recorded the traditions which he heard.

antagonistic camps. In 1662 this interloper was turned out and a Churchman instituted. A secession took place and the present Congregational Chapel, then called Independent, at the top of the High Street, was founded. The air was electric.

It was that very same year, in which by God's providence John Ray came to Glastonbury and saw the tomb in the ruined chapel. Later in that year, tradition says, from fear of Puritanical fanaticism like that which destroyed the Holy Thorn, silently, hastily, at night, the altar tomb was removed from the ruined shrine in St. Mary's Chapel at the abbey, and placed in the churchyard of the parish church for protection outside the east End of St. Mary's chapel in that church. And there it remained till the autumn of 1928, when loving hands brought it reverently into the church and placed it in the ancient St. Katherine's chapel, the north transept. The tomb was generally known as the John Allen tomb. The Rev. Thomas Warner, in his well-known history of Glastonbury, ascribes it to Thomas Allen. It may have been so called to protect it. Anyway it bears the initials of Joseph of Arimathea on it—J.A., with a caduceus between them. There could be no badge more suitable for the Messenger of Christ to this country than the caduceus, the badge of Mercury, the messenger of the gods. It is an official badge which would not be put on a private person's tomb. And to this day the Patriarchs of the Eastern Church carry a caduceus instead of a crozier being carried before them. When the stone top was taken off the tomb on its removal, the following was evident. *It was a moved tomb and a tomb that had been moved in haste, as the tradition had said. For wherever metal clamps had held the stones together, they were missing, and the stones were badly broken there.* Moreover, there is a plinth inside to receive the silver ark with the saint's remains. On the top are the stumps of the uprights of the feretrum or metal grill on which pilgrims hung their offerings, and which guarded the relics.

A glass top was put on the tomb, that all generations might see what was found. It is a deeply carved and dignified tomb, and its appeal is great after 266 years in the rain and frost. Some still cling to the belief that it is John or Thomas Allen's tomb. Most of us think that we have here an altar tomb which sheltered for a time the remains of him who gave up his own tomb for Christ and found a tomb in far-off Britain, and brought that country to the feet of Christ—the very shrine before which the pilgrims knelt.

APPENDIX 3

KINSHIPS OF THE HOLY FAMILY

IT will surprise most people to know that in the English
College of Arms, the Heralds' Office, there is a pedigree
of Christ and His relatives from Adam downwards. It is
both in chart and narrative form. The pedigree of Our
Lord's immediate family is startling. It is strange to find
it there. It is Roll 33, Box 26. Interest centres in St. Ann
and her sister Bianca. Ann had three husbands: first,
Joachim, by whom she had the Blessed Virgin Mary;
second, Cleophas, by whom she had another Mary who
married Alphaeus and who was the mother of St. James
the Less, Symeon (St. Simon), St. Jude or Thaddaeus, and
Joseph Barsaba,[1] who are generally called "the Brethren
of Our Lord", thus making them cousins of the half-blood.
It is very startling that the third husband attributed to St.
Ann is Salome (usually the name of a woman). By him she
had a third Mary,[2] and it is equally startling that she is

[1] Many expositors think that Judas Barsabas and Joseph
Barsabas were brothers. (Barsabas has many explanations,
amongst others "Son of Wisdom".) Bishop Lightfoot suggests
that they were brothers and that the former was St. Jude the
Apostle. (Like St. James the Less, Joseph was called Justus.)
These opinions and suggestions fit in with the statements in
the above pedigree very well. Dr. William Smith in his
Dictionary of the Bible mentions that some ancient MSS. call
St. Jude Zelotes (as his brother St. Simon was called) and sub-
stitute the name Thaddaeus for Jude in the list of the Apostles.
[2] "Mary Salome" figures prominently in the French tradi-
tions of those who came in the boat to Marseilles with St.
Joseph of Arimathea, but, unlike him, remained and died in
France.

said to have married Zebedee and was the mother of St.
John the Divine and St. James the Great, thus making
them also cousins of the half-blood to Our Lord. Bianca,
St. Ann's sister, had a daughter Halisbert (our Elizabeth)
who married Zacharias and who was the mother of St.
John the Baptist, thus making him second cousin to Our
Lord, as in the Bible. There was evidently some tradition
for it to be enrolled in our College of Arms, that St. John
and St. James were half-cousins to Our Lord, and that his
" brethren " were really half-cousins. The pedigree throws
light on many a vexed point. But one must record that
the narrative of the same Roll shows a somewhat different
pedigree. It makes "the brethren" of Our Lord half-
brothers, St. Mary (not St. Ann) marrying Cleophas after
St. Joseph's death. St. Ann is only given two Marys as
daughters, she marrying only Joachim and Salome, but
St. John and St. James, the sons of Zebedee and Mary, are
still half-cousins of Our Lord. In these very ancient pedigrees, as they come to us, one must expect slips, but there
must have been some tradition for this relationship of the
two Apostles to Our Lord to be recorded.

But this is not the only English record. In the Harl.
MSS. in the British Museum, 38–59, f. 193b, there is a des-
cent of both the Blessed Virgin Mary and St. Joseph from
David, making Heli, the father of the Blessed Virgin, and
Jacob, father of St. Joseph, to be brothers, thus making St.
Mary and St. Joseph first cousins. (St. Matthew makes
Jacob and St. Luke makes Heli the father of St. Joseph.)
The pedigree skips many generations just as Welsh pedi-
grees often did. (And so do Jewish: St. Matthew gives
forty generations, and St. Luke fifty-six, from Abraham to
St. Joseph.) This pedigree refers to the pedigree in St.
Matthew, i, 16, and St. Luke, iii, 23, for Heli and Jacob,
and to St. Peter's claim in Acts ii, 30, and St. Paul's in Acts
xiii, 23, and Romans i, 3, that Our Lord came of the line

of David. But besides this attempt to reconcile the Biblical genealogies by making the Blessed Virgin and St. Joseph first cousins, it makes St. Joseph of Arimathea uncle of them both, and his daughter Anna consobrina or cousin of the Blessed Virgin, thus surpassing the usual Eastern tradition.

Another MS. in Jesus College, MS. 20, makes Anna mother of Penardin (a somewhat Cornish name) who married King Lear,[3] and so was mother of Bran the Blessed and grandmother of Caractacus, thus linking the Holy Family with the ancient British Royal Family. I am indebted to Mr. Edward Hepburn of Monkridge, Sidcup, Kent, for these extracts from the Heralds' College Roll, the Harleian MS. and the Jesus College MS. Their great value is that they record some traditions. There is some fire behind the smoke. The smoke blinds sometimes. But there is fire behind it.

To sum up, the Heralds' College MS. throws a new light on the relationships of that little band of Christ's followers that changed the history of the world. The Harleian MS. supports the claim that Joseph of Arimathea was uncle of the Blessed Virgin, and making St. Joseph and St. Mary first cousins makes him uncle of them both. It also claims that he had a daughter Anna, calling her Consobrina, or cousin, of the Blessed Virgin Mary. The Jesus College MS. makes this Anna have a daughter Penardin who married

[3] As stated in the text, Anna, daughter of St. Joseph of Arimathea, is said to have married King Beli, and here we have a claim that King Beli's grandson King Lear married Penardin daughter of St. Anna. We do not claim accuracy for these ancient pedigrees, especially Celtic ones, but here are two claims that members of the Holy Family married two celebrated British kings, Beli Mawr the Great and King Lear. That there was one or more such matches is probably the basis. Perhaps Welsh scholars can say whether one of these names is the generic name for a king.

King Lear, and so links with the British Royal Family.
The dates make this possible. We remember the striking
Palue, or Parlooe, tradition giving St. Anna of royal
Cornish blood a first husband in Cornwall, and a husband
in Palestine of the race of David: it makes one wonder
whether Penardin was the daughter of St. Anna by a
Cornishman in Cornwall, or by a Jew settled there, as so
many Jews did, notably at Marazion. Nor can we forget
that King Arthur, and indeed every one of the Knights
of the Round Table, claimed descent from St. Joseph of
Arimathea. So many Welsh traditions and pedigrees claim
various descents from intermarriages with the line of the
ancient British kings, and some relative of the Blessed
Virgin. If there was any connection through trade or blood
between St. Joseph of Arimathea and King Arviragus, it
explains the friendly reception of the former by the unconverted King.

It is perhaps worth mentioning that the *Protevangelium*,
the apocryphal gospel, claiming to be written by St. James
the Less, describing the birth of Christ, makes St. Joseph
a widower when he married the Blessed Virgin, and calls
St. James " the cousin and brother of the Lord Jesus " in
its title. SS. Chrysostum and Cyril, and others, believed in
the authenticity of this gospel. If St. Joseph and St. Mary
were cousins as stated above, St. James would be half-
brother and cousin of Our Lord. The gospel must be very
old. It is frequently quoted and it calls St. James " Chief
Apostle and first Bishop of the Christians in Jerusalem ".
It must pre-date the claim that St. Peter was the chief
Apostle.

It may also interest readers to know the descent of King
Arthur from St. Joseph, given by John of Glastonbury.
One should add that, while " Nepos " often means grand-
son, it may merely mean kinsman.

Helaios or Nepos of Joseph
|
Josue
|
Aminadab
|
Castellors
|
Manuel
|
Lambord
|
A son
|
Ygerna
|
Uther Pendragon
|
King Arthur

It is said that every one of the twelve Knights of the
Round Table was descended from St. Joseph.

A FEW SALIENT DATES OF GLASTONBURY ABBEY

A.D.

37 or 63	Wattle church built.
167 or 183	Mission of Fagan and Dyfan. St. Michael's on Glastonbury Tor built.
450 (about)	St. Patrick first real Abbot.
470 (about)	Gildas the Wise enters Glastonbury Abbey.
488	St. Bride comes to Glastonbury.
540	King Arthur buried there.
540 (about)	Maelgwyn tells of St. Joseph's burial there.
546 (about)	St. David builds on a chancel to the wattle church.
603	St. Paulinus, St. Augustine's companion, enclosed the wattle church with wood, and leaded the roof.
688	King Ina "timbered a Minster of Glastonbury". (*Winchester Chronicle*.)
704	King Ina laid his Charter on the altar of his Lignea Basilica (wooden church).
725	King Ina handed over Glastonbury Church to Rome (132 years after St. Augustine came).
728	King Ina died at Rome where he had founded the present English College.
950 (about)	St. Dunstan extended King Ina's church.
1184	Destruction of the wattle church by fire.
1185	Norman Chapel of St. Mary built on site of the wattle church, and Church of SS. Peter and Paul begun.

A.D.

1190 (about)	Galilee finished, and King Arthur's and Queen Guinevere's bodies found.
1278	King Arthur's and Queen Guinevere's remains moved to the new church.
1350 (about)	Abbot Walter Monington extended the choir by two bays.
1534	The Edgar Chapel (begun by Abbot Richard Bere) finished by Abbot Richard Whyting.
1539	Abbey dissolved, and Abbot Whyting hanged on the Tor.

HISTORIANS OF GLASTONBURY

(PRE-REFORMATION)

Name and Date	Periods covered in their history
	A.D.
MAELGWYN OF LLANDAFF About 540 (possibly Maelgwyn of Avalon, 1st century)	About 37–82
WILLIAM OF MALMESBURY A.D. 1129–1135	37–1135
ADAM DE DOMERHAM About A.D. 1295	1135–1290
JOHN OF GLASTONBURY About 1400	1290–1400
WILLIAM OF WORCESTER'S *Itinerary* Visited, about 1478	1475–1480
JOHN LELAND'S *Secretum* or *Chartulary* 1534	1534

OUR LORD'S TRADITIONAL VISIT TO BRITAIN

I HAVE dealt under "Traditions" with the one that Our Lord came when he was a lad with St. Joseph on one of his expeditions to Britain, and how others have searched for confirmation of this startling tradition. I am here going to say a few words dealing with attempts to discount it. Some people openly call it a myth. The sad thing is that some of them create myths to try to disprove it. I have dealt with such a mythical explanation. Unfortunately for the Dignitary and his informants, whoever they were, I learn from the indefatigable Rev. H. A. Lewis that Mrs. Weeks, postmistress of Priddy, told him:

(*a*) That Mark Simmons who died aged about 90 in 1933, and used to teach in Sunday School and Chapel, would suddenly say to his hearers, " Suppose you saw Jesus coming up the hill again now."

(*b*) Mrs. Barker, widow of a former Vicar, often referred to His coming.

(*c*) The Rev. W. H. Creaton, Vicar in 1904–1919, later Rector of Yeovilton, Yeovil, had spoken of it.

(*d*) Many old folk did so when she was a girl.

So we may feel that the Dignitary and his informant or informants have unconsciously created a myth to disprove what they considered one.

True, that Prebendary Palmer, Vicar of East Brent, son of a former Vicar of Priddy, when a lad, has said that neither he nor his brother ever heard the story. That is

not surprising. Young men in their holidays think more
of cricket, and football, and skating, generally.

I may add that the Rev. H. A. Lewis, on sending his
little book *Christ in Cornwall* to Mrs. Wardell-Yerborough,
widow of a former Vicar of Tewkesbury about 1935,
received in a letter of thanks from her, an expression
of surprise that he had not quoted a proverb still used in
the Mendips, " As sure as Our Lord was at Priddy." She
wrote from the Mendips.

APPENDIX 6

THE LATE
MR. FREDERICK BLIGH BOND, F.R.I.B.A., AND
THE ARIMATHEAN TRADITION

THERE is a guide book, entitled *Guide Book to Glastonbury Abbey*, being sold, to which the name of no author is attached and no date, but which claims to be " Revised by F. Bligh Bond, F.R.I.B.A.". There are very plain signs that it is an old guide book, brought up to date by someone who knows his subject very well, but yet falls into considerable inaccuracies. For instance, the statement on p. 54, that the gateway to the women's almshouses bears the date 1512, shows clearly that that was written many years ago. In 1910 that date was quite clear in embossed though worn figures. In 1921 it was just legible. For many years past now the rain has completely obliterated it. There are also statements in the guide-book such as " The plan of it represents a cruciform church, *square at the east end* " (p. 30) a statement which Mr. Bligh Bond fiercely battled against to the end. Again, " William Wyrcestre (William of Worcester) describes a grand entrance porch of which no vestige remains " (p. 32). Mr. Bligh Bond discovered the foundation of this porch about 1910, and clearly marked it out on the green sward. That dates this edition of the guide-book as comparatively recent. The statement about the letters on the gateway points to a much earlier edition of this guide-book, which doubtless Mr. Bligh Bond revised years ago. The statement about the square end of the great church shows that this book was re-edited after or during

164

Mr. Bligh Bond's visit to America. The Committee of Inspection appointed by the Council of the Somerset Archaeological Society (under whom Mr. Bligh Bond excavated) reported on May 13, 1910: " We consider that there was sufficient evidence in the appearance of the ground on the north side, when it was laid bare, to justify the construction of a wall to mark the outline of the trench. On the south side enough masonry was found to put the fact of the existence of a wall beyond dispute." This is the minute of the Somerset Archaeological Society.

In addition to the above quotations from the guide-book which date the separation between its earlier and present editions, there appears an amazing statement, to those who knew Mr. Bligh Bond, who is announced as revising that guide: " a few particulars relative to the traditional burial of St. Joseph of Arimathea here, will no doubt be interesting to the reader. It is evident that Malmesbury did not believe in this legend: his name occurs but once in the chronicle. This is most inaccurate. The whole of William's Chapter 1 is taken up with the coming, doings, and death of the members of the Arimathean mission, as Chapter 2 is with the coming of the next mission 100 years later and their finding the church built by the first mission, and their settling in the same spots, which they inhabited.

The above quotation was shown to the author of this book. As it was in a book supposed to be revised by Mr. Bligh Bond, whom he had known intimately for nearly a quarter of a century, he at once wrote to Mr. Bond expressing his amazement. Mr. Bond, in reply on a postcard, wrote: " Feb. 20, 1945. Underwent operation Dec. 6 and still in hospital, but hope to write fully soon. . . . My immature *Guide* has been out of print for over twenty years." He collapsed suddenly and died about a week later in his eighty-second year. Only in June 1944 he had written to the author asking for several copies of his next edition, and added: " Could you let me have a copy of your current edition as I have not got it here? I might annotate it for you, as I have some new matter myself." (Alas, it was not sent.) This shows Mr. Bond's sympathy, always warmly expressed for over twenty-three years, with the Arimathean tradition. But, let us quote his own words in the " Author's Foreword " in his latest book, *The Mystery of Glaston*: " The Glastonbury tradition, which is our priceless national heritage, may be concisely stated thus: The Church in Britain was the earliest organized church in Western Europe. It was founded in the last year of the Emperor Tiberius—about A.D. 37—by Joseph of Arimathea and a company of twelve, at a place now known as Glastonbury. . . . Britain thus claimed not only a National Church, not subject to foreign jurisdiction, but a privileged position in the Councils of the whole Church Catholic, and this was accorded her."

Mr. Bond was particularly keen on the position accorded to the English Bishops at the Councils of Pisa, Basle, Constance, and Sienna, because Joseph of Arimathea had brought the faith to Britain " immediately after the Passion of Christ ".

"JOSEPH WAS IN THE TIN TRADE"

IN addition to the testimony of the late Henry Jenner, F.S.A., of the British Museum, on the above subject, in a letter to myself, and in the *Quarterly Review* of the Benedictines of Caldey, 1916, Mr. Jenner gave further evidence on the subject in an article in the *Western Morning News*, April 6, 1933. There he tells that he was dining some forty years before at the house of a former Harrow Master, Mr. George Hallam, who told him that he had just heard from a friend of his, Mr. James Baillie-Hamilton, an amateur in organ building, who went to the workshop of one of the principal London organ builders to see how metal pipes were made. To obtain a perfectly smooth and well blended surface, a shovelful of molten metal is thrown along a table on which a linen cloth is stretched, an operation demanding peculiar skill. Each workman before he made his cast said in a low voice, " Joseph was in the tin trade ". After some persuasion the foreman told Mr. Baillie-Hamilton words to this effect: " We workers in metal are a very old fraternity, and like other handicrafts we have our traditions amongst us. One of these, the memory of which is preserved in this invocation, is that Joseph of Arimathea, the rich man of the Gospels, made his money in the tin trade with Cornwall. We have also a story that he made voyages to Cornwall in his own ships, and that on one occasion he brought with him the Child Christ and His Mother and landed them at St. Michael's Mount." Mr. Jenner went on that he had heard before that the saying " Joseph was in the tin trade" was current in Cornwall, but had not seriously considered which St. Joseph was referred to. But next day when he went to the British Museum he looked up St. Joseph of Arimathea in the *Acta Sanctorum*; he found nothing there about the tin trade, but he found the usual stories from the Gospel of Nicodemus, the Glaston-bury Traditions and the Grail Legends. But he did find in one life the story that St. Joseph accompanied St. James the Great to Gallicia in Spain, the other tin district of that period. Incidentally Mr. Jenner in the same article tells that shortly after hearing the Baillie-Hamilton story, he was staying at South Uist in the Outer Hebrides and found a whole set of legends of the wanderings of the Holy Mother and Her Son in these islands.

On April 13, seven days after Mr. Jenner's article, there appeared a letter in the *Western Morning News* that a Cornish woman, whose father was a miner and brought up in a mining village, remembered the songs and carols sung by children. One of them began " Joseph was a tin merchant, a tin merchant, a tin merchant ", and described his arriving from the sea in a boat. Is it too late to recover the words of this song?

Mr. Jenner mentions in his article that he told the Baillie-Hamilton story to his friend, Mr. Arcott Hope Moncrieff, the editor of Black's *Guide to Cornwall*, who inserted it in his 1895 edition. I am indebted to the inde-fatigable Rev. H. A. Lewis for this further information about Mr. Henry Jenner.

WAS THE BLESSED VIRGIN MARY BURIED IN ST. MARY'S, THE OLD WATTLE CHURCH?

It is well known that Church dedications to St. Mary did not begin much before 1130. But apparently St. Mary's, Glastonbury, was an exception. True, we do not hear of the dedication before William of Malmesbury wrote about 1135, but he wrote then as if during all its history it had been so called. He speaks of the many saints, "Some of whom we shall notice in our progress" (and these lived centuries before 1135) " who there awaited the day of resurrection under the protection of the Mother of God." I had at first thought that St. Mary's, now popularly called St. Joseph's from the shrine of its builder in its crypt, had followed the usual early course and been named after its founder, and that about 1135 its dedication had been changed like so many others to St. Mary's. I cannot think so after considering William of Malmesbury's above-quoted words. The earliest dedications were generally to the Blessed Trinity, St. Michael, or some saint who probably was buried on the spot. This great exception of an early dedication to St. Mary is another reason that makes me wonder if she was buried there. In the text of this book I have touched on the recollections of the old banished priest, William Goode (who had served in this church as a child) and his vivid remembrance of the words " Jesus, Maria " carved on the outside southern wall. He describes them as "carved in stone in characters of great age". I have also raised the point of the word " super " (over) in the

most ancient writing that we have about Glastonbury
(Melchinus or Maelgwyn, about A.D. 540) which tells of the
burial of St. Joseph close to St. Mary's Chapel—"juxta
meridianum angulum oratorii cratibus preparatis 'super'
potentem adorandum Virgininem supradictis spherulatis
locum habutantibus tredecim". The word "spherulatis"
has been the puzzle which has occupied the minds of
many. It is a past-participle. "Sphera" is a "circle".
All sorts of far-fetched interpretations have been given.
Doctor Armitage Robinson called the whole passage from
which this is taken an "age-long" puzzle. It seems to me
that the simple meaning "encircled" is the best interpretation of "spherulatis". I venture then to translate this
portion of the passage (which relates to the burial place of
St. Joseph of Arimathea) thus: "Next to the south corner
of the house of prayer, made of prepared wattles *over* the
adorable powerful Virgin by the aforesaid circle of thirteen
inhabiting that place." To speak of the anchorites dwelling
in huts as encircled is quite natural both here and at Iona.
St. Joseph came with his eleven companions, hence the
twelve Hides of land given to them. But this passage
speaks of thirteen inhabiting the spot. Was the thirteenth
the Blessed Virgin? I have pointed out in the text that
Pynson's *Metrical Life of St. Joseph* is consistent with the
possibility that the latter was here fifteen years with the
Blessed Virgin and after her koimesis—falling asleep (later
"assumption")—his charge over, he went into France to St.
James, and later came back here. That might also account
for the two dates strongly insisted on for his coming, A.D.
37 and A.D. 63. The church would be built by the circle of
thirteen, and at the end of the first period, the Blessed
Virgin be buried there. I have commented in the text on
the others laid in the sanctity of the little church, and the
extraordinary claims set forth for it. But I must just lay
stress on something else, this time from Malmesbury's *Acts*

of the Kings. It occurs in a passage which I have quoted at
the end of all editions of this book. But in my quotation
there are two gaps for the sake of brevity, marked by
dotted lines. The passage omitted in the last gap succeeds
these words (translated): "The very floor, inlaid with
polished stone, and the sides of the altar itself above and
beneath, are laden with the multitude of relics." Then follow
these words (translated): "where also one can notice in the
pavement stones are carefully set side by side, either in
triangularly or squarely and sealed with lead, under which
*if I believe some sacred secret to be contained I shall not
do an injury to religion*" (ubi etiam notare licet in
pavimento, vel per triangulum vel per quadratos lapides
altrinœcus ex industria positos, et plumbo sigillatos, sub
quibus quiddam arcani sacri contineri si credo, injuriam
religioni non facio).

What secret? In the final passage which I have omitted
William refers to his book on the *Antiquities of Glastonbury,* so it was after he came and learnt its full story that
he wrote thus. As it had become a duty to believe in the
Assumption, the words of William which I have marked
by italics bear a special meaning.

I may add here, that there is some show of probability
that the expression "Secretum Domini" applies in one
instance, to the private chartulary of the Lord Abbot, but
that does not wipe out the tradition that the expression
"the Secret of the Lord" is a name for Glastonbury. This
passage tends to give strong corroboration to the name.

THE CLOSE CONNECTION BETWEEN BRITTANY AND BRITAIN

THE more one thinks of it, the more one is convinced of the extent of the influence and activity of the Celtic Church, sacrificed, as its Master was, for political and racial reasons, but, like Him, surviving, and risen again with a more glorious body. It was swamped for a time by the Church of the Mistress of the World, but it finally broke loose, re-assumed its missionary activities, and is in every sense catholic, all over the world. The following facts I have condensed as I find them stressed by Thomas Taylor, M.A., F.S.A., in *Celtic Christianity in Cornwall*, pp. 50–52. They substantiate and enlarge what I have written about the very close connection between Brittany and Cornwall. He tells how the Romano-British settlement in Brittany, A.D. 387, turned the Gaulish language of Brittany into a Romano one, but how the 4th- and 5th-century flooding of Brittany from Cornwall, increased by the foundation of the Kingdom of Wessex in 519, was so great that it destroyed the Romano language and produced Breton.

The Cornish, Welsh and Breton languages were closely akin, but the Breton and Cornish closer together. In this century the language spoken in Finistere, Morbihan, and Cotes du Nord, is modified Cornish. He shows that apart from names of local places the very divisions of the land tell the same tale. The part between the Elorn and the Elle in Brittany was actually called " Cornouaille ", and the part between the Elorn and the Cuesnon was called

" Dumnonia "—the early name of Cornwall, Dorset, and
Somerset. Although the sea divided them, Cornwall was
more akin to Brittany than to Wessex. But Mr. Taylor
does not stop there. He stresses how Breton nobles and
knights accompanied William the Conqueror, glad to spoil
the hated Saxon. Richard Fitz-Turold received thirty-one
manors, Brient six, Blohire five, Jovin thirteen, Wihumar
three, and Judhel one, in Cornwall. So complete was the
union between the two countries that nearly 500 years later
the first subsidy roll of Henry VIII shows that more than
one-sixth of the tax-paying population of the Hundred of
Penwith were Bretons—tinners, fishermen, smiths, ser-
vants, labourers, and cooks, and twenty-nine people of no
occupation. And in the church register of Camborne,
starting in 1538, these settlers are entered as " Brito ",
" Bryton ", or " Brytton ". Bretons as such still contributed
handsomely to subsidies in Cornwall in 1599. In those days
the two peoples were akin not only in race, and traditions,
but in their religion. It was not till the days of John Wesley
that this religious race, separated politically from Brittany
suddenly swerved to Nonconformity, to which there is now
in some parts a reaction. The Church in Cornwall, Somerset and Wales in the early days remained the Celtic Church
(retaining such things as the Celtic Easter and Tonsure).
Mr. Taylor tells how the Celtic Church in Wales and Ireland sent its missionaries to their fellow Celts in Brittany
after Cornwall was cut off from Wessex. Welshmen were
founders of the following Breton monastery-bishoprics:
St. Pol Aurelian, Lumaire, Magloire, Mewan, and Malo.
Tutwal, who founded Treguier, was from Dumnonia.
There are about 200 names of British saints, which still
linger in the parish place-names and holy places of
Brittany: of these, some eighty to ninety are Welsh.
There are about sixty in Cornwall. About thirty to forty
names of British saints occur only in Brittany, Cornwall,

and Devon. And there are a few in Somerset. And later, Breton saints, like SS. Aurelian, Sampson, Columba, Meriadec, Corentin, and others, were venerated in Cornwall. So completely did the two countries absorb the traditions and mode of worship of each other.

ARCHBISHOP USSHER'S ACCOUNT OF THE GLASTONBURY TRADITIONS

SEEING the misuse that has been made of slight portions of the celebrated Archbishop Ussher's (of Armagh, 1581–1656, primate of Ireland) story of the Glastonbury Traditions, it may be worth while to state what authorities he quotes. His *Antiquities of the British Churches* is a sealed book to many, as he wrote in Latin. But Mr. H. Kendra Baker, of Hindhead, translated it as a result of the publication of the first edition of this book. Ussher published it in 1639 in Dublin. He devotes the whole of his second chapter to the Church of Glastonbury Traditions.

(1) He begins by quoting William of Malmesbury's *The Antiquity of the Church of Glaston*, telling how after the persecution in St. Stephen's time, St. Philip the Apostle settled in France, and sent twelve disciples to Britain, of whom the chief was St. Joseph of Arimathea, "his dearest friend", and how the King (Arviragus) and two successive Kings (Marius and Coel) gave them Ynniswitrin (Glastonbury) from which fact the twelve Hides of Glastonbury take their name, and how they were inspired by a vision of St. Gabriel to build a church of twisted wattles in honour of the Blessed Virgin Mary in the thirty-first year after Our Lord's Passion, and the fifteenth after the Assumption of the Blessed Virgin, i.e. A.D. 63.

(2) He tells how Cardinal Baronius quotes from *The Acts of Mary Magdelene and her Companions*, telling how dur-

ing the persecution after the death of St. Stephen, the Jews, in their hatred, placed Lazarus, Mary, Martha, and Marcella, their attendant, in a boat without oars which floated down to Marseilles. He adds how Baronius tells from a MS. History of England, in the Vatican Library, " that their companion was St. Joseph of Arimathea, who, they relate, sailed from Gaul into Britain and, thereafter preaching the Gospel, ended his days ".

(3) He cites the *Chronicle of Pseudo-Dexter* that in the year of Christ 48 " the Jews of Jerusalem, being violently hostile to the blessed Lazarus, Magdalene, Martha, Marcella, Maximin, Joseph of Arimathea the noble decurion, and many others, put them in a ship without oars or sails, and without a rudder, and ordered them to live in banishment, who divinely carried by the mighty ocean reached the port of Marseilles uninjured ".

(4) In a fragment attributed to Heleca, " It is said that Magdalene the sister of Lazarus with Lazarus, Maximin and Chelidonius, Marcella and Joseph of Arimathea, came into Aquitanian Gaul, and there preached the Holy Gospel of the Lord Jesus, as the histories of Gaul clearly teach, and is the generally accepted tradition of that region."

(5) He also cites Freculphus, Bishop of Lisieux, 815–845: " Moreover that which Freculphus, cited by Malmesbury, holds concerning the apostleship of Philip in Gaul, is expressed word for word in the book of Isidore concerning the Fathers of each Testament, for in each we read that Philip preached Christ to the Gauls and that he led barbarous nations and near to darkness, and bordering on the swelling ocean, to the light of knowledge and to the gate of faith." Ussher proceeds to express his dissatisfaction (recorded in the text of this book) with Baronius's substitution of the word " Galatians " for " Gauls " in the above passage from Isidore Archbishop of Seville, A.D. 600–636, which Freculphus quotes.

(6, 7, and 8) He says that the above Isidore in "The Fathers of each Testament" (cap. 74) and in the Liturgy of Toledo (the Gothic ᵒ ᵈd Mozarabic Liturgy), in Festo St. Jacobi and Tom. 2, and Julian Archbishop of Toledo on the Prophet Nahum (col. 205), and the author of *Collections and Flowers* (Bede?, Vol. 3) all assign Gaul to St. Philip, who is also said " to have preached Christ to the Gauls in the book on the Feasts of the Apostles which is found in the MS. of the martyrology of Hieronymus (Jerome). This Hieronymus is probably the contemporary of St. Victor of Rome who was martyred A.D. 193.

(9) He quotes verses from Capgrave (1393–1454), "In Vita Josephi" from the *Tabula Magna Glastoniensis*, and from the Appendix to the *Chronicon Glastoniensis* in the Cottonian MS., to show the firm belief held then in the mission to Glastonbury by St. Joseph, his son Josephes, and ten others, and in the grant of the twelve Hides of Glastonbury. The *Chronicon* also says that St. Philip ordered St. Joseph to go, that King Arviragus refused to believe in Christ, but gave the twelve Hides, that " Joseph left the rights with those companions, in the 31st year after the Passion of Christ, and that these men built a Church of Wattles ". St. Joseph is said by Cressy to have died at Glastonbury in A.D. 82. The above might mean that he died in A.D. 63–64.

(10) He says that " to-day " (1639) there is to be seen at Wells in the house of Sir Thomas Hughes of the Order of Knighthood, a bronze tablet formerly affixed to a column in the Church of Glaston with this inscription on it: " In the year 31 after the Lord's Passion 12 holy men, of whom St. Joseph of Arimathea was the chief, came hither and built the 1st Church of this Kingdom in this place, which Christ at that time dedicated to the honour of His Mother, and as a place for their burial."

(11) He mentions as in the possession of Lord William

Howard, son of Thomas Duke of Norfolk, "a remarkable tablet comprising the antiquities of Glastonbury"—the Magna Tabula—"which tells that St. Joseph of Arimathea and his son Josephes were baptized by St. Philip, and became his disciples, and that St. Joseph was appointed by St. John, toiling exclusively at Ephesus, 'paranymphos' (attendant) to the Blessed Virgin Mary, was present with St. Philip and other disciples at her assumption, and came fifteen years *after the assumption* with Josephes to St. Philip in Gaul, *then* came to Britain (as told in the book called *The Graal*) promised to him and his seed, with his wife and son Josephes whom the Saviour Himself had previously consecrated to be Bishop in the City of Saraz." And he quotes "wonderful stories in the life of Joseph which Capgrave relates in his most frivolous book which is called *The Holy Graal*."

He then refers to a vision shown by an angel to a hermit concerning Joseph of Arimathea and the Holy Graal "out of which the Lord supped with His Disciples", and gives a description of it recalling the dish out of which Arabs feed today. According to Vincent Bellovacensis, whom Ussher refers to, this vision was in the second year of Leo III, A.D. 719. He says that "Thomas Malory has transferred many things into the fabled *Acts of King Arthur* put forth by him in the English tongue, who here makes use of the word 'Sangreal' very closely approximating to the idea of the True Blood." Ussher says that Malory "represents a portion of the most precious blood of our Saviour to be here preserved, either shed on the Cross, or reserved as the Last Supper of Christ." He further tells that Forcatulus says that "the Britons record that Joseph brought with him a pledge and witness of that sacred Supper."

(12) He refers to several other authors, an important one of whom is the learned historian Polydore Vergil (referred

to in the text), Archdeacon of Wells, who lived 1470–1555, of whom he says, "Polydore Virgil, a man of greater sagacity after dismissing the grosser fables of the monks, thus sets forth this history [Book 2] : 'That Joseph, who on testimony of the Evangelical Matthew, born in the City of Arimathea, had buried the body of Christ, whether by chance or design, came by the Will of God, with no small retinue into Britain. . . . These men, assuredly inspired by the Holy Spirit, when they accepted of the King a little piece of land for their habitation (nigh to the town of Wells about 4000 paces). Here they laid the first foundations of the new religion. . . . The name of the place is Glasconia. This constituted absolutely the first beginnings of the Christian faith in Britain, which later on, though nearly extinguished, King Lucius rekindled—being sustained by the fountain of baptism—and piously augmented, as we shall hereafter relate. For Gildas is witness that the British received the Christian religion from the very beginning of the rise of the Gospel.'"

(13) He quotes Thomas Hatfeldius in the *Summary of the Kings of England* as telling how in the time of good King Lucius, SS. Faganus and Duvianus (or Deruvianus) found an ancient church built by the Disciples of Christ, with ancient writings to the effect that, after the Holy Apostles had dispersed to preach, St. Philip coming into France sent twelve of his disciples into Britain, of whom Joseph of Arimathea was the chief.

(14) He also quotes " a letter in the name of our Great Patrick (composed by the monks of Glastonbury—that is the charter of the Blessed Patrick quoted above by Malmesbury), in which concerning the origin of the Church, which by the Anglo-Saxons is called Eald-circ, that is the Old Church, in treating of it it is thus introduced. The Brothers have produced to me the writings of SS. Phaganus and Deruvianus in which it is recorded how that 12 disciples

of SS. Philip and James built the Old Church itself in
honour of our foreordained advocate angel Gabriel. And
moreover, that the Lord divinely dedicated the same
Church in honour of His Mother, and how that three
pagan Kings gave these twelve, twelve portions of land for
their support." He also quotes Malmesbury as to the grant
of the twelve Hides by these three pagan kings in A.D. 63.

(15) He quotes Domesday: "The Church of Glastonbury hath in its own domain (villa) 12 Hides which have
never paid tax."

(16) He says that Capgrave in his *Life of Patrick*, Tinmuth, and Harding, said that the twelve Hides were given
by King Arviragus, but that Capgrave in his *Life of Joseph*
says that they were given by the three kings in succession,
Arviragus, his son Marius, and grandson Coillus or Goel.
He adds that John Harding hardly admits that the three
kings were pagans, but that Arviragus was converted by
St. Joseph, and baptized, and that Marius and Coillus
"were to some extent imbued with the Christian religion,
although they did not partake of that perfection which
was meet".

Richard Vitus of Basingstoke is quoted as saying "that
Arviragus was well affected towards the Christian religion.
Coelus also, his grandson by his son Marius, was 'instructed
in the Christian religion for a short time while he
(Arviragus) lived, not however that he professed it
publicly.'"

Ussher adds: "From Juvenal indeed it appears that
Arviragus became King of the Britains while Domitian
was Emperor, since our Joseph is said to have died under
Vespasian in the year 76."

(17) The Archbishop quotes Nicholas Sanders and Fox
and Gildas the Wise as telling of the coming of St. Joseph
in the reign of Arviragus, and founding the Church here,
and Sanders as saying "in the 50th year of Christ, for so

Gildas the Briton, a Christian writer, who on account of his surprising erudition was called 'The Wise', related nearly 1100 years before our time." (N.B.—Gildas gave the year 38.)

(18) Archbishop Ussher in a footnote gives the celebrated passage beginning "Joseph of Arimathea, nobilis Decurio" and attributes it to "Melthinus (or more properly Mewynus) who was before Merlin". He also quotes the passage about " Abbadare mighty in Shaphat ", evidently referring to pre-Christian days. Both these quotations refer to St. Joseph's burial in the bifurcated line next to the corner of St. Mary's Chapel and of the silver and white cruets with the blood and sweat of Christ, buried with him. He also refers to the history of the " Cross of St. George ", and how St. Joseph gave it to King Arviragus "for the insignia of the British race ".

(19) He has much on the claim of priority for British bishops at the Councils of Pisa, Basle, Constance, and Sienna, gives account of rival claims, and tells how Sir Robert Wingfield, Henry VIII's ambassador to the Emperor Maximilian in 1517, caused the account to be published from the recorded "Acts of the Council of Constance itself"—and tells where the MSS. copies were, one in the Royal Library, and the other in Sir Henry Wootton's.

(20) The Archbishop gives a copy of the licence given by Edward III in 1345 to John Blome of London to go to Glastonbury and dig for the body of St. Joseph beneath the enclosure of the monastery if he gets the licence and assent of the abbot and chaplain. It is signed by the King himself, June 8. He states that he copied it from the royal archives in the Tower of London. He records that a chapel was dedicated at the abbey to St. Joseph, and that his tomb was there.

(21) He then gives the narrative of William Goode the

Jesuit, who in the reign of Henry VIII was born at Glastonbury and was educated there as a boy. This is the narrative
dilated upon by Dean Armitage Robinson to throw doubt
on the claim that St. Joseph was buried in Glastonbury.
It begins, "There were in existence at Glastonia inscribed
tablets of brass to perpetuate his (St. Joseph's) memory,
chapels, crypts, crosses, arms, and the observance of the
feast of St. Joseph for six days at the Kalends of August,
as long as the monks enjoyed most securely the King's
Charters: now all things have perished, mingled with
the ruins." This is quite enough to show plainly that the
monks thought and taught that St. Joseph came to
Glastonbury, which is the important thing. Later, William
Goode records seeing the brass plate on a stone cross (over-
turned under Queen Elizabeth I) telling of the coming of
St. Joseph and his companions, of King Arviragus's permission to dwell at Glastonbury; of the two silver cruets
with the blood and water from Our Lord's side; of the
denoting of the size of the wattle church; of the stone
bearing the words "Jesus Maria" and of the arms of the
abbey—with the two cruets under the arms of a cross on
a shield sprinkled with blood-drops. He ends, "These
were always denominated the insignia of St. Joseph, who
was piously believed to have lived, and probably to have
been buried there."

Ussher then quotes the "Record of the Burial of St.
Joseph and his companions" from *The Great Register of
the Monks of Glaston*. He then adds the words of a monk
of Malmesbury in the second book of his *Eulogy*, already
quoted. He then adds that William Goode also wrote the
extraordinary words, "But none of the monks ever knew
the exact position of this holy sepulchre or described it.
They say that it was most carefully concealed, either there
or on a mount, which is in the vicinity of a pointed mountain, and the name of which is Hamdon Hill." This is

Hamdon Hill near Montacute, some eighteen miles to the south of Glastonbury. As I have said, " After all, the important thing is the life of St. Joseph and not his burial." But these extracts from Ussher are alone enough to support the claim that St. Joseph was buried at Glastonbury. And there is no warrant to support Dean Armitage Robinson's suggestion that his coming was uncertain. And it is to be noted that in Sir Robert Wingfield's *Record of the Transactions of the Council of Constance* these words occur: " To whom [St. Joseph and his companions] the King assigned 12 Hides of land in the Diocese of Bath for their maintenance, who, so it is written, are buried in the Monastery of Glastonbury in the Diocese of Bath "—a claim, as Ussher shows, as old as Melchinus or Maelgwyn who was before Mewyn or Merlin, and repeated constantly —" next to the corner of the Oratory over the adorable Virgin ", close to Joseph's well. It is just possible that the monks of Goode's day had forgotten where the body was found 200 years before, ere the remains were put in his shrine, which was the result of the search by John Bloom. But before their eyes was the sarcophagus in the shrine, the constant pilgrimages to it, and the ceremonies of the feast in August there. To go on pilgrimage to Joseph of Arimathea as executors were sometimes ordered to do, was to go to his shrine at Glastonbury. From prehistoric days there was the claim of his burial there. But, after all, the important thing is his coming, not his burial.

WILLIAM OF MALMESBURY

Such plausible, and sometimes wild, statements have been made about what William wrote, that it is advisable to say a few words.

William was a monk of Malmesbury. His writings became so famous that the monks of Glastonbury invited him to go and stay there, and write the history of their celebrated abbey. This he did in 1129. Among his very many books were (1) *The Acts of the Kings of England* written about 1120, (2) *The Acts of the Bishops of the British* which he wrote in 1125. Of these two books he wrote later editions between 1135 and 1140. In his first book about the Kings, he referred to Glastonbury and attributed its foundation to the Eleutherian Mission (about 183). After he had lived at Glastonbury and seen its Library and heard its Traditions, he altered this, and in his *Antiquity of Glastonbury* (1121) traced the foundations to a mission sent by St. Philip from France, of which he writes, " their leader, it is said, was Philip's dearest friend, Joseph of Arimathea, who buried Our Lord." Later, in Cap. 2, he wrote of the Eleutherian Mission: "They also found the whole story in ancient writings how the holy apostles, having been scattered throughout the world, St. Philip the Apostle coming into France with a host of disciples, sent twelve of them into Britain to preach, and that —taught by revelation—constructed the said chapel which the Son of God afterwards dedicated to the honour of His Mother."

He also wrote of the Eleutherian Mission: " Preaching

and baptizing, they went through all the parts of Britain until they reached the Isle of Avallonia. . . . There God leading them, they found an old church built, as 'twas said, by the hands of Christ's disciples, and prepared by God Himself for the salvation of souls, which church the Heavenly Builder Himself showed to be consecrated by many miraculous deeds and many mysteries of healing." And later, in the same chapter, he wrote: " These twelve therefore abode there in divers spots as anchorites, in the same spots indeed which the first twelve inhabited." Clearly William wrote of two distinct missions separated by about one hundred years.

William was a very careful historian. Archbishop Ussher calls him " our chief historian ". John Leland calls him " an elegant, learned, and faithful historian ". William says of himself, " I deem it necessary to acquaint him (the reader) that I vouch nothing for the truth of long-past transactions, but the consonance of the times; the veracity of the narration must rest with the authors. Whatever I have recorded of later times I either have myself seen or heard from credible authority. However in either part I pay but little respect for the judgment of my contemporaries, trusting that I shall gain from posterity, when love and hatred shall be no more, if not a reputation for eloquence, at least credit for diligence." Such was our author, a reliable, careful historian.

When he wrote *The Antiquity of Glastonbury* he followed these principles. He quotes Freculphus, Bishop of Lisieux in France, 825–851. (It is most interesting to find that Freculphus's book is in the Catalogue of Glastonbury Library in 1248, so that William almost certainly saw it.) William writes:

" Now St. Philip, as Freculphus testifies in his 2nd book, chapter IV, coming into the country of the Franks to preach, converted many to the Faith, and baptized them.

Therefore, working to spread Christ's word, he chose twelve from among his disciples, and sent them into Britain to bring thither the good news of the Word of Life, and to preach the Incarnation of Jesus Christ after he had most devoutly spread his right hand over each. Their leader, it is said, was Philip's dearest friend, Joseph of Arimathea, who buried Our Lord."

With what he had learnt at Glastonbury in his mind, when he made a later edition of his *Kings of England* he altered what he had written in the first edition, sometimes writing in whole passages from *The Antiquity*. It was only natural. He did not know the Glastonbury story when he wrote his first edition of *The Kings*. Glastonbury was of sufficient importance to have to be mentioned, but it was only a rough sketch. Now, with his greater knowledge, he felt bound to be more detailed and accurate. So he did that very difficult thing. He did not re-write everything. He incorporated. It is interesting to see what he did say in his later edition. He retells the Eleutherian Mission. But he adds the record of the Arimathean one. This is what he wrote: "Moreover there are documents of no small credit, which have been discovered in certain places, to the following effect: 'No other hands than those of the Disciples of Christ erected the Church of Glastonbury. Nor is it dissonant from probability, for if Philip the Apostle preached to the Gauls as Freculphus relates in the 4th chapter of his second Book, it may be he believed that he also planted the Word on this side of the Channel also.'"

Will it be believed that some of the gainsayers of our beautiful Glastonbury Tradition airily say that when William wrote his later edition of *The Kings* he said nothing about the Arimathean Tradition? One despairs of the mentality of such critics.

It is true that the MS. of William's *Antiquity of Glas-*

tonbury which is in Trinity College Library, Cambridge, and was transcribed in its original Latin by Thomas Hearn in 1727, has in it events which took place after William's death in 1142, such as the fire which burnt up the monastery in 1184, and a list of abbots at the end right up to the Dissolution in 1539. These are patent additions which have crept into this MS. They do not justify people electing to reject portions that come within the period of William's lifetime, because it suits their theories to do so.

As a matter of fact, there are marginal notes in the MS. in another but very old hand such as a passage which John of Glastonbury tells us comes from *The Acts of the Illustrious King Arthur* (by Gildas Badonicus 516–570), another very long note on St. Patrick by another and later hand, and another note of ancient but different date and in later ink about Arthur's burial, and yet another referring to Adam de Domerham's *Chronicle*. MSS. were scarce and precious, and students sometimes added to them without any idea of fraud, as in all these cases. If anyone seriously wants us to reject any passage in Malmesbury's *Chronicle*, let him either produce evidence of a different handwriting, or of the impossibility of its being William's own.

THE GLASTONBURY TRADITION AND THE PRECEDENCE OF ENGLISH AMBASSADORS

IT is well known that at the great Church Councils of Pisa, 1409, Constance, 1417, Sienna, 1424, and Basle, 1434, precedence was accorded to English Bishops on the ground that Joseph of Arimathea brought the Faith to Great Britain " immediately after the Passion of Christ " (" statim post passionem Christi "). This Tradition was held as of such great importance that immediately after the invention of printing, when books were so scarce, the story of St. Joseph of Arimathea was printed. The great Wynkyn de Worde himself printed a *Life of St. Joseph*, and John Pynson in 1516 and 1520 two other Lives.

Another proof of the great importance this story was considered to be is that while the claims of the English bishops at all the aforesaid Councils were insisted on (that is during the reigns of Henry IV, Henry V, and Henry VI) it was not till the reign of Henry VIII, just 100 years after the Council of Constance, that Sir Robert Wingfield, the English ambassador, had all the findings of the Council of Constance on the subject carefully recorded in a book as Archbishop Ussher tells in his *Church History* (Cap. 2) in the reign of Elizabeth and the Stuarts. In the Archbishop's time one copy of the book (published at Louvain in 1517) was in the Royal Library, and another in Sir Henry Wotton's. It may be of interest to record the names of some of the Church dignitaries at these Councils. At Pisa, 1409, the English delegates were Robert Hallam, Bishop of Salisbury, Henry Chichele (Archbishop of Canterbury in

1414) and Thomas Chillenden, Prior of Christ Church, Canterbury. Hallam was the leader. So he was at Sienna in 1417. With him there was Nicholas Bubwith, Bishop of Bath and Wells, and the Bishop of St. David's. The celebrated Cardinal Beaufort, then Bishop of Winchester, joined them later. He had been Dean of Wells. Nicholas Frome, Abbot of Glastonbury, was a delegate at Basle in 1434.

But attention has lately been drawn to the fact that not only English bishops but English ambassadors claimed precedence on the very same ground—the Glastonbury Tradition. Queen Elizabeth I claimed it, and in her claim refers to the fact that her father claimed it. Recently there appeared in a book-seller's catalogue notice of a Pamphlet of 1642 for sale, which Lord Queenborough promptly secured for the Royal Society of St. George. It is called *A briefe Abstract of the Question of Precedency between England and Spain.* It goes on to say that it was "occasioned by Sir Henry Nevile Knight the Queen of England's Embassador and the Embassador of Spain." The claim was pleaded "before the Commissioners appointed by the French King who had moved a Treaty of Peace in the two and twentieth year of the same Queen" —1579. It is of special interest that this claim was recorded again in this Pamphlet dated 1642, when nothing could be printed without a licence and that during the Commonwealth it was reprinted in 1651 in Cotton's *Posthuma.*[1] So the Sovereigns of England publicly insisted on the precedence of their representatives from Henry IV till Elizabeth, and Charles I and Oliver Cromwell gave a licence for this claim to be recorded and published—a claim based on the writing of Gildas the Wise (born 425)[2] the first British historian, who had lived for a time in

[1] Sir Robert B. Cotton's *Posthuma,* 3, 7, 77.
[2] *Vide* p. 160.

Glastonbury Abbey, and had known its records and traditions.

This unbroken claim recalls the spirit of Henry VIII's reminder to the Pope that William the Conqueror had refused to do fealty to the then Pope on assuming the Crown of England, following in the steps of the Saxon Kings. And what was the claim put forward in the Pamphlet of 1642 (p. 3), *Precedency of England in respect of the Antiquity of Christian Religion immediately after the Passion of Christ in this Realm*"? The same claim for the ambassadors and in the same words as the claim for the bishops in the four great Church Councils, an age-long claim which had not been forgotten even through turbulent times when men grasped simple essentials.

In conclusion the Reverend Paul Stacy, late Vicar of St. Peter's, Coventry, has pointed out that in the next century under an engraving of Glastonbury Abbey in the year 1733, now in the Abbey House, these words occur: "it is certain that from a belief in that Tradition the Ambassadors of England take place of ye Ambassadors of most Kingdoms in Europe as representing ye Kingdom that was soonest converted to Christianity." The same claim all down the centuries! It has been reserved for modern critics to throw easy doubt on an age-long claim. Thus they embalm themselves. To quote from memory either Alexander Pope, or Dryden on critics:

"Pretty in amber to see dirt or flies or dust or straw,
    The things themselves are neither rich nor rare—
    One wonders how the devil they got there."

THE CELTIC CHURCH

IT is very difficult to write a short account of the Celtic Church. But it must be done. For nothing is more pathetic than that, in spite of the glorious missionary zeal of the saints of that Church, the memory of it and of them has been nearly forgotten. As mentioned in the text, this is mainly owing to political events. The constant raids of the heathen Saxons, their demolition of churches, monasteries, and manuscripts, coupled with the driving of the Britons into mountains and morasses, and, after the Saxons were converted, the similar raids by their still heathen kinsmen, the Danes, nearly wiped out the Christian Church in this land, except in portions of Western England. And then gradually, in spite of vehement Celtic resistance, by the 8th century the overwhelming Continental influence of the Roman Church, tremendously reinforced later by the Norman Conquest, and derived from the prestige of Imperial Rome's position as Mistress of the World, at last caused the memory of the Celtic Church, and her courageous saints, to be nearly eclipsed. But their deeds do follow them; they are the foundation of the English Church; forgotten of men, they themselves are treasured in the Paradise of God. The Church of this land owes its persistence to the great flood of faith, like a mighty silent ocean, which flows from its earliest history. Fortunately in recent years a wave of remembrance is surging up, and Glastonbury and Iona, and the whole Celtic Church, are coming into their own. It is only possible to be very brief here. Anyone who wants to learn more should read, among other books, Dr.

W. Douglas Simpson's *The Celtic Church in Scotland* and *They built upon a Rock* by Diana Leatham (Celtic Art Society), a resourceful and informative book from which very many details in this short account are derived. By " the Celtic Church" one means the Church of Britain, Gaul, Scotland, and Ireland.

There is nothing more striking in the history of the early Church than the way in which the individual Churches came to each other's aid, and had intercourse with each other—in fact, were one. All sprang from Jerusalem, but the great Churches of the East, Africa, Rome, and Celtica, were one. It is a marvellous history. The cruel persecution which led to the placing of St. Joseph of Arimathea and his companions in the sail-less and oar-less boat was at once the seed both of the Gallican Church in the Rhone Valley, and of the Church in Britain, side by side with the preaching of St. Philip and St. James, and other Apostles, and they were the parents of the Churches of Ireland, Scotland, America, and the British Dominions. Just as in God's providence the captivity of Joseph in Egypt welded the whole national life of the Jewish nation, so in the 5th century A.D. the heart-breaking six years' captivity of the Christian British lad St. Patrick, in Ireland, led ultimately to the glorious conversion of the whole of Ireland and Scotland—although, nearly half a century before him, St. Ninian had founded a little Church at Nendrum on Mahee Island in Strangford Lough. One has recorded in the text of this book some of the missionary activities of the Celtic Church on the Continent, even in the 1st century. All that one has space for here is to give a short account of a very few of the other great Celtic missionary saints, and to say a few words about them, emphasizing not only their great energy and zeal, but that orthodoxy which, as we have seen in the text, was praised by the great St. Athanasius.

The Celtic Church was great in monasticism. In monasteries were trained the missionaries. The bishops often lived in them and, unless they were abbots as well, submitted themselves to the abbot. The monastic system was largely developed by the African Church in Egypt. St. Anthony was the great promoter of it. He was very vigorous, and at the age of eighty-seven walked to Alexandria to support St. Athanasius. In A.D. 330 St. Athanasius visited the monastery of Pachonius, an Egyptian Monk. In A.D. 404 St. Jerome translated Pachonius's rule. When Imperial Rome fell in 410 Palladius records that in the region about Thebes in Egypt alone there were 7,000 monks. Illustrious bishops of all Churches fostered them; e.g. in Asia, St. Hilary; in Gaul, St. Martin of Tours; in Italy, St. Ambrose; in Africa, St. Augustine of Hippo. To the above-mentioned St. Martin of Tours, maternal great-uncle of the Briton, St. Patrick, can be directly traced the enormous development of monasticism and the missionary work of the Celtic Church. He was by birth an Italian pagan. He was formerly an officer in the Emperor Constantine's army. He came across St. Hilary, who converted him. In A.D. 351 the Arians banished both him and St. Hilary. He became a hermit at Milan and then at Liguge. At the latter he founded a great monastery, which grew so that it was called Marmontier or "Big Family". This became the great pattern of all the Celtic monasteries. Like the anchorites at Glastonbury and Iona, they lived in separate huts or caves, or cells. St. Martin was still at Liguge in 371. In that year he became the celebrated Bishop of Tours.

St. Ninian, a Briton educated at Rome, went to live at Marmontier under St. Martin. He was the great link in the general spread of the monastic system from the Continent to Britain. He was an ardent missionary to the Picts of Scotland. He found at Marmontier a copy of St.

Jerome's translation of the New Testament, the Psalms and the Mosaic Law. From these he carried a copy of the Vulgate to his celebrated monastery, Candida Casa, which he founded at Whithorn in Scotland. Later St. Finbar made a copy of it at Candida Casa. St. Ninian's church at Candida Casa, where he was buried, was dedicated to his old master, St. Martin. And, just as St. Martin's tomb at Tours was a place of pilgrimage, so did St. Ninian's at Candida Casa become. St. Ninian died in 432. He had founded Candida Casa in 397, exactly 200 years before the mission in 597 of St. Augustine from Rome to re-convert South-Eastern England, overrun by the pagan Saxons. It is interesting to note that Candida Casa submitted to the Roman Church in 730, the same period as that in which King Ina of Wessex handed over Glastonbury, founded in A.D. 37, to Rome. Ninian's death occurred in the same year as St. Patrick landed at Strangford Lough on his great mission which resulted in the conversion of all Ireland. St. Ninian was succeeded as abbot of Candida Casa by St. Caranoc. Our records of the work and wonderful illuminations and MSS. of the great Celtic Church are mainly preserved to us through Ireland, which escaped the Saxon raids (though not the Danish), and through Bobbio in Italy, founded by St. Columbanus, the great Celtic missionary, who died there in 615.

At Bobbio there were preserved in the Library the beautiful illuminations and MSS. of Candida Casa, and of (the Irish) Bangor. Many of the 700 MSS. kept there are in Celtic script. Some are now in Turin and Milan with notes in Brito-Pictic script by St. Columbanus himself, and his companion, St. Gall, who left Bobbio, and went on to found the monastery of St. Gall in Switzerland. Space fails to tell all the journeys and voyages of these irrepressible and daring Celtic saints. Suffice it to name a few and tell of some of their doings.

(1) St. Caranoc the Pict. Caranoc succeeded St. Ninian as second abbot of Candida Casa in Scotland in 432. He succeeded St. Ninian and resigned his post to go on his last mission to Ireland, to a settlement of St. Ninian's on Stratford Lough, about which we shall soon have to say a few words.

(2) St. Patrick the Briton. In the text we have spoken of his parentage, birthplace, and place of burial. But he cannot be quite left out here because of the immense importance of his missionary work in the Celtic Church. We would just add that his real name was Succat, and that the name Patricias or Patrick means " of noble birth ". Professor Hewins in his *Royal Saints of Britain*, in a pedigree, names his sister Darerca as the wife of Conan " Meriadec " Duke of the Armorican frontier (a Roman office) under the Emperor Maximus, who is said to have been the first King of the Bretons. She is also called great-niece of St. Martin of Tours. The difficulty is—who gave St. Patrick the name of Succat? For he was carried away captive to Ireland when about sixteen. The amazing thing is that the *Book of Ballymote*, and the *Book of Lecan*, both say that he, the son of a deacon and grandson of a priest, was baptized during his captivity by Caranoc above mentioned, who was at a Christian settlement at Nendrum in Stratford Lough. It is more likely that St. Patrick the slave somehow came across Caranoc, who, as we know, was on his last mission to Ireland, and that he influenced him for good, and led to his great repentance. Baptism in those unsettled days was sometimes amazingly delayed. The Christian Emperor Constantine the Great was not baptized till on his death-bed, twenty-five years after his conversion; St. Ambrose not till his thirty-fourth year; St. Augustine not till his thirty-second; both the latter were born in Christian families, and were convinced and keen Christians.[1]

[1] Dean Stanley's *Eastern Church*, p. 216.

We know from St. Patrick's "Confession" in the *Book of Armagh* that St. Patrick had not taken advantage of all the Christian teaching in which he had been brought up, and that like the Prodigal Son this was brought home to him by his misfortune. It is possible that the story of the two books may have some light thrown on it by the horrid fact that when he was about to be made bishop someone disclosed a sin of his early youth that he had confessed before being made deacon and that some bishops, unwilling that one so unlearned should be consecrated, used it as an excuse. But even then, if he was careless, or wild, how came it that the son of a deacon and the grandson of a priest was unbaptized? St. Patrick was always full of repentance for a wasted youth and the neglect of opportunities, educational and otherwise. His own words were "Before I was afflicted, I was like a stone which lies in the deep mire." But what a precious jewel for Christ the stone turned out to be! The first part of his captivity was in the Wood of Lochlut, "the oldest wood that ever was in Ireland, and the gloomiest". There he made friends with little children who were kind to him. In return, he, prayerful, and fully repentant, tried to convert them. In consequence he learned Gaelic, and the ways of the Irish, so useful to him when he came on his mission. These children always lived in his affectionate heart. Afterwards in Ulster, as a slave to Milchu, he taught other children at Glemish in Antrim. After his escape, and landing at Marseilles, on his way to his friends in England, he made for Tours where his great-uncle, St. Martin, was consecrated bishop in 371. He passed through Auxerre where St. Germanus was consecrated bishop on July 7, 418. St. Patrick is said to have been born about 395. He was sixteen when taken captive. He was a slave for six years. If these dates be right he would have been free about 416. But there is no certainty about the date of St. Patrick's birth.

So it is quite possible that he found that most remarkable man Germanus on his episcopal throne. Germanus's biographer, Constantius, who wrote forty years after his death, records that Germanus died July 31, 448. In 429 he and his fellow Gallican bishop, Lupus of Troyes, in response to an appeal from the British Church, was sent by a Gallican synod to Britain to fight the Pelagian heresy and, as it turned out, to win the Alleluia victory (Smith and Wace's *Christian Biography under Germanus*). Whether St. Patrick had known St. Germanus before or not, William of Malmesbury tells us that Germanus, after the victory, took him into his own suite of followers. He is said to have learned more from St. Germanus than from anyone else. It seems that St. Patrick was advised by St. Paulinus of Lola to study on the island of Lerin near Cannes, but exactly when is not clear. One thing is certain: Palladius was sent to Ireland by Pope Celestine in 431. He was a failure, and died after a few months. Immediately, in 432, St. Germanus, who saw St. Patrick's worth, consecrated him at Auxerre, and sent him to take Palladius's place, where his charm, courage, and knowledge of the Irish succeeded. He bearded King Leary at Tara itself. He won permission to preach throughout his kingdom. Conall, one of the King's brothers, was converted and built St. Patrick a church at Donaghpatrick, whence he spread the Faith through Meath. He destroyed the chief idol of Ireland. In seven years he built fifty churches in Connaught. He built the church at Armagh, which became the Archiepiscopal See. He established monasteries for monks and nuns all over the land. He taught through Leinster and Munster. He became Archbishop of Ireland, and his See remains to this day. He had entered Ireland as a slave. He left it as Archbishop to return to the Mother Church of his native Britain, there to gather the successors of the first anchorites under one roof, and to die blessed and beloved of all, as William of Malmesbury tells us (Caps. 8, 9 and 10).

(3) St. David the Briton. St. David of Wales's great work is recognized, though far too nebulously. He was a perfect pivot, and centre. Men from all parts came to him, and he at a moment's call was ready to undertake a journey, and link together places so far apart as Glastonbury and Jerusalem. St. David was son or grandson of Ceredig, Prince of Cardigan. He was born at Menevia (now St. David's). He is said to have been uncle to King Arthur. The date of his birth is uncertain, the dates varying between 542 and 601. The latter must be much too late, and probably the former too, for he collaborated with, amongst others, St. Columba, St. Gildas, and St. Finnigan. What is known is that he became Archbishop of one of the three ancient British Archiepiscopal Sees, Caerleon on Usk, and that he removed the site of it from there to his birthplace Menevia. It is also known that he presided at the Synod of Brefi which condemned the Pelagian heresy, that he much encouraged monasteries, and founded one in the Rhos Valley near Menevia. He is said to have been trained under Paulinus. William of Malmesbury, writing in 1129, tells us St. David was the first to build a chancel to St. Joseph of Arimathea's wattle church at Glastonbury. He speaks of him as " that great man " and tells several tales about him, and his love for Glastonbury, and his veneration for St. Patrick. He gives an account of his activities at Glastonbury, his gifts to it, and his visions there. Amongst other stories he tells how after a vision in his monastery in the Rhos Valley he set off next day with two monks to Jerusalem to aid the Patriarch beset by foes, whom his preaching converted. William says of him: " This worthy saint of God died in A.D. 546." He calls him " this holy and incomparable man ". As we speak of other saints, some of his activities, and his wonderful influence

and attraction, will be seen. Pope Calixtus II canonized him centuries after, in 1120. The activities of these people are so wonderful, William of Malmesbury who tells of St. David's wish to build on to the Old Church and of the pillar that he put to mark its original dimensions, tells also how Paulinus encased it with wooden panels and lead from top to bottom. He tells how St. Columba of Iona came to Glastonbury. And when one reads that St. Brendan of Clonfest visited St. Columba in Iona, and St. David at Menevia, it will be seen how these sailor saints travelled as well as built monasteries, and held consultations. It was for the Glory of God, and to spread Christ's Kingdom.

(4) St. Finnigan of Clonard, another Irish Pict educated in Britain, who died at his Abbey of Clonard in 549, who made constant journeys to St. David at Menevia in Wales, and who introduced into Ireland the Liturgy drawn up by St. David of Wales, St. Gildas of Glastonbury, and St. Cadoc of Candida Casa in Scotland. St. Finnigan appointed twelve Apostles of Ireland among whom were St. Columba who founded Derry in 546 and Iona in 563. Another was the zealous Irish priest St. Kenneth who, after wonderful work in Scotland, founded Achabo in Queen's County, Ireland, in 578.

(5) The princely St. Columba of Iona, at once a preacher, poet, artist, great organizer, a patron of arts to whom Scotland, and ultimately the North of England, owe their conversion. He was an Irish Scot, and spent the first forty years of his life in Ireland. He was paternally a descendant of the old Irish kings. As a young man he entered the monastery of Morville under the great Irish Pictish saint, St. Finbar. Later he became a monk at Clonard in Meath under the great St. Finnian. In 546 he founded the monastery of Derry. Later he founded Kells, so celebrated for the illuminations in the *Book of Kells*. St. Columba is alleged to have founded 100 monasteries in Ireland.

Although lovable and tender-hearted, he was of a fiery
disposition, and this led to such a serious civil war that as
a penance he was told to emigrate to Scotland. He did so
and at once started evangelizing the Scots of Alba, and
finally in 563 founded the great community of Iona,
whence his monks founded settlements in the cities of the
West. We get a glimpse of him leading a party of pilgrims
to pray at the tomb of St. Martin of Tours. He died in
597, the very year that St. Augustine landed on his mission
to Kent. His name is had in remembrance, and his works
do follow him.

(6) St. Kentigern, nicknamed St. Mungo. We first hear
of him as a monk under St. Fergus at Cannock. He was
there ten years. But on St. Fergus's death the monks took
his body in a bullock cart and trekked and buried him in
a cemetery long before consecrated by St. Ninian of
Candida Casa, near Glasgow, and founded a monastery
there and called it Glasgu (happy family). Persecuted
Christian Britons fleeing from the Saxons took refuge there.
At length, years later, King Roderick of Strathclyde, aided
by, among other allies, St. Kentigern's grandfather Urien,
a local chief, in 575 won the battle of Arderyd, near
Carlisle, over pagan Solway Britons, Angles, and an exiled
Irish-Scottish chief, Prince Aedham. This victory consolidated the North Britons as a nation, and gave peace to the
Church. King Roderick wished St. Kentigern to be head
of the Church there, and according to Celtic custom he was
consecrated by only one Irish bishop. Joceline gives an
account of the ceremony and how the bishop arrived with
a Pastoral Staff of simple wood, and dressed in the roughest
hair cloth. There was a great difference between the lives
of the missionary bishops and the more luxurious bishops
of the towns. At Glasgow, like St. Anthony, St. Martin
and St. Ninian, they dwelt in separate huts, as they did at
Glastonbury until St. Patrick brought them under one roof.

After seventeen years as abbot there, St. Kentigern quarrelled with Markon, a local chief who helped Roderick to win the battle of Arderyd. The chief threatened St. Kentigern's life and eventually killed Urien, Kentigern's grandfather. St. Kentigern fled south with the intention of joining the Christian Britons in Wales. On the way he ministered to Christian Britons of Cumberland driven into the hills by Northumbrian Angles. There he founded a Christian settlement, whose crosses still remain: Mungriesdale, named after his nickname, is one. At length St. Kentigern arrived at Menevia in Wells, where St. David had been archbishop for seventeen years. St. David used his influence with a good pagan, King Maelgon, who allowed St. Kentigern to build a monastery at Llanelwy (now St. Asaph) named after St. Kentigern's immediate successor. St. Asaph's is equally distant from Whithorn in Scotland (Candida Casa), St. David's in Wales, and Bangor in Ulster. St. Congall's community in Bangor had 3,000 monks, Picts, Britons, Gauls, and even a few Teutons. The custom both at St. Asaph's and Irish Bangor was for one-third monks to work, one-third to grow food, and one-third to pray each day. Divine service went on day and night.

After King Roderick in 575 had won the said battle of Arderyd, he sent messengers to St. Kentigern to return. The latter enthroned St. Asaph as his successor at Llandwy and went. Roderick met him at Hoddon near Annan in Dumfries-shire. From Hoddon, till Glasgow was ready to receive him, the saint formed new monasteries at Lanark, Peebles, and at St. Mungo. Then, when at Glasgow, he planned a great mission to Aberdeenshire. Two Welsh disciples, St. Tinan and St. Nidan, accompanied him. St. Tinan and St. Nidan began the foundation of four monasteries. They were afterwards sent back to Wales, and founded the monasteries of Llanfidan, and Llanidan in Anglesey. When too old to go himself he planned missions, and sent his monks to the Orkneys, Shetlands, Norway, and Iceland. St. Ninian had introduced the title Papa (Pope) for the heads of monasteries more than 100 years before. And the names Papa Westray in the Orkneys, and Papa Stour in the Shetlands for islands is a relic of monastic missions over there. A 9th-century Danish author says: " Before Iceland was colonized from Norway, there were men living there whom the Northmen called Papas: they were Christians and it is thought that they came over the sea from the West, for after them were found Irish books and bells and croziers and other things, so that one would see that they were Westmen."[2] Such was their zeal and energy and daring. For " the love of Christ constrained them ".

(7) St. Columbanus. or Columban, was born about 540. He was an Irish Pict. After thirty years in Ireland at Irish Bangor, doing Christ's work, he set out together with St. Gall to the Continent, he to found the monastery of Luxeuil in the Vosges, St. Gall later from there to found that of St. Gall in Switzerland. They clung to the Celtic time of keeping Easter. This scandalized the Gallican clergy, who had lapsed from that custom. St. Columbanus vigorously fought the Pope on this subject and the Gallican bishops, who wished him to give it up. He wrote to the Pope[3] " and boldly told him that he was astonished that so learned a man as he has not remedied the patent error of the Gallican Church, and that it was well nigh heretical to disagree with the great scholar St. Jerome, who, be it noted, praised the system of calculations followed by the Celtic Church ". He was left in peace and so long as he lived at Luxeuil continued to keep the Celtic Easter. In 602, twelve Gallican bishops held a Council at Chalons, and bade him appear before it. He refused, and wrote

[2] *They Built upon a rock*, by Diana Leathem, p. 129.
[3] *They Built upon a rock*, by Diana Leathem, p. 171.

saying, " I trust more to the Traditions of my native country than to Victorius who writes ambiguously and denotes nothing."

Theuderic, King of Burgundy, for a personal quarrel, banished St. Columbanus back to Ireland. But the saint went back to Luxeuil. He was then deported to Nantes. On the way Agiluff, the Teuton, King of Lombardy, asked him to settle in Northern Italy and he crossed the Alps. St. Gall was too ill. They parted. St. Gall founded the monastery called after him in the mountains near Lake Constance in Italy. (One of the Christian kings of Lombardy is said to have sent all his nine daughters on pilgrimage to Ireland, because of St. Patrick.) During his stay at Milan, St. Columbanus at once attacked the Arian heresy and urged the Pope to call a Synod. He wrote to Pope Boniface IV. " Does the Pope condemn or condone this action of his predecessor Vigilius? [who re-admitted the heretic Nestorius and his companions to the Church]. Let him make his position clear, for if he ' condones ' Vigilius, then those who have preserved the faith have a perfect right to judge the Pope." Thus was he valiant for the Faith. Such was the fierce orthodoxy of the Celtic saint. St. Columbanus then restored a little church at Bottio dedicated to St. Peter. King Clothan sent a messenger from Luxeuil, begging the saint to return to his kingdom. But the saint because of his age felt the journey too much, and so he remained at his wonderful monastery at Bottio. where years after St. Francis of Assisi came, and got his inspiration there. He borrowed from there for his monks the title " Soldier of Christ ", the same uniform, the same outlay, the wooden cross at the entrance, and the Celtic name "Curcaie" for their caves. Never had Christ two braver, more consistent, outspoken soldiers. St. Columbanus died in his beloved monastery at Bottio in 615.

(8) St. Brendan the Scot was a hardy sailor missionary. He worked among the Picts of the Western Isles of Scotland, and founded many Christian Settlements in them. He visited Iona about 545, some twenty years before the great St. Columba made his great settlement there. He founded Clonfert in Ireland, and laboured among the Picts of Perthshire as well. He visited not only his great successor in Iona, but St. David at Menevia in Wales to give him the latest news of that wild North, where St. David had worked as a missionary before the Scots and the Angles had invaded it. He also gladdened the heart of St. David by telling him how the Irish Picts from the celebrated and more ancient monastery of Candida Casa founded by St. Ninian in 397 had come to his aid in the Western Isles. Among the early Christians there was neither Pict nor Scot, bond nor free, but, Christ was all, and in all.

(9) St. Bride of Kildare. Before we come to that very great saint, St. Cuthbert, who witnessed and had part in, at least by acquiescence, the absorption of the Celtic Church of Britain into the English Church under the Saxon kings, we ought perhaps to retrace our steps and consider the wonderful work of the great Abbess of Kildar in Ireland. The date of her birth is uncertain. Some say that she was born after St. Patrick's death, others that she came to Glastonbury a few years after his death; others tell a very pretty story of what happened when St. Patrick was professing her.[4] William of Malmesbury says definitely that she came to Glastonbury in A.D. 488, and returned back to Ireland. Her father was Dubtach, a pagan Scottish Kinglet of Leinster, her mother a Christian Pictish slave. Just before St. Bride's birth, her mother was

---

[4] St. Patrick by mistake had used the form for ordaining priests. Someone told him of it. He replied, "So be it, my son, she is destined for great things."

sold as a slave to a Druid landowner. St. Bride remained
with her mother in the West till she was old enough to
serve her legal owner Dubtach, her father. It is told that
as a child her mother took her to hear St. Patrick preach,
an event apparently never forgotten by her. As she grew
up she was marked by her high spirits and tender heart.
She could not bear to see anyone hungry or cold. She had
at once to relieve their distress, and this led her to give
away things that were Dubtach's. When Dubtach pro-
tested, she replied that "Christ dwelt in every creature".
Practically all the Celtic Saints were distinguished for their
love of animals and of nature. It is remarkable what a
number of stories showing this still linger. Incensed at her
attitude, Dubtach went to sell her to the King of Leinster.
While waiting for the completion of the bargain, she gave
a treasured sword of her father's to a leper. Infuriated,
Dubtach was about to strike her. Bride said that she had
given the sword to God through the leper, because of its
great value. The King, a Christian, forbade Dubtach to
strike her, saying "Her merit before God is greater than
ours." Dubtach, thus hindered, solved the problem by
giving St. Bride her freedom. She at once went and told
her mother, who was old and in charge of a dairy of her
master's. Bride took charge, and, unchanged, gave away
some of the produce. But the dairy prospered so under
her, that the Druid gave her mother her freedom. St. Bride
returned to her father, and left her mother peaceful and
free. Dubtach arranged a match for St. Bride with a young
bard. Bride refused, and to keep her virginity, went to
Bishop Mel, a pupil of St. Patrick's, and at length she took
the first vows. She became the Patron Saint of all milk-
maids, and at Glastonbury she is twice over sculptured
milking a cow—in the 12th century, on the glorious north
door of St. Mary's Chapel, and, in the 14th, over the doorway on the ruined Chapel of St. Michael on the Tor. She

was a great traveller, hence her name St. Bride of the Isles.
In her first nunnery she started with seven nuns. At the
invitation of bishops, she started nunnery after nunnery
all over Ireland, amongst them St. Patrick, St. Finian, St.
Fiacc, who wrote St. Patricks life, and Erc, St. Brendan's
helper. Nothing stayed this wonderful little woman. She
traversed mountains, bogs, forests, vile roads, and seas.
Her monastery of Kildare on the Liffey was for both
monks and nuns. Combeth, noted for his skill in metal-
work, became its first bishop. Cogitusus, a monk in it,
wrote the life of St. Patrick, and of St. Bride, in the 7th
century. St. Bride died February 1, about 525.

It was St. Bride who invented the double monastery.
Another great abbess, St. Hilda of Whitby, developed it
later. St. Hilda had intended to enter the French monastery
at Chellis. It was the great St. Aidan, Bishop of Lindis-
forne, who on one of his missionary journeys dissuaded
her. How right he was in his judgment is shown by the
fact that at the Synod of Whitby, held in her convent at
Whitby in 663, out of sixteen bishops in Britain, five had
been trained by her. Beside St. Bride's visit to Glastonbury,
where she had built a church at Beckery about half a mile
off, and where after she had left the people built a bigger
one dedicated to her, there are two other things linking
her with Glastonbury Abbey. One is a message to St. Gildas
the Wise, who, driven by Danish pirates from the Isle of
Steepholme, had taken refuge in Glastonbury Abbey as an
inmate, but had afterwards got permission to return to his
hermit's life close by. St. Bride sent a messenger to Gildas,
asking him to make her a bell, which he did. The story,
as told by a monk of Rwys in Brittany in his *Vita Gildas*[5]
about A.D. 860, using earlier documents, is worth repeating
as showing the great abbess's and contemporaries' venera-

[5] Translated from the Latin by the Rev. Hugh Williams for
the Hon. Society of Cymsidosion, London, David Nutt, 1901.

tion for St. Gildas. " Now St. Bridget, an illustrious virgin
who lived and flourished in the province of Hibernia, and
presided as Abbess over a Nunnery, on hearing of the
renown of Gildas, sent a messenger to him, saying with
enticing words ' Rejoice, holy father, and be always strong
in the Lord. I beseech thee to deem it worthy to send me
some token of thy holiness that the memory of thee may
ever without ceasing be held in honour among us '. Then
Gildas, having heard the holy virgin's ambassador, made
with his own hands a shape of wrought work, and composed a bell (propriis manibus formulum fecit fusili opere,
et tintinabulum composuit) and despatched it to her by
means of the messenger whom she had sent. She joyfully
took it, and gladly received it as a heavenly gift sent to her
from him."

The other link is that when she left Glastonbury,
William of Malmesbury tells us[6] that she left behind " a
victual bag, a necklace, a bell, and embroidery implements
which are there treasured in her memory ". He wrote this
600 years later. They were still there 400 years later, till
the Reformation, being shown as relics. Until within the
last decade (very few years ago) an ancient Celtic bell,
believed to be her bell, was kept in Glastonbury, and struck
every year (it had lost its clapper but had a lovely tone) on
the feasts of the three great Celtic saints connected with
Glastonbury, St. Bride's, St. Patrick's, and St. David's, in
St. Patrick's Chapel attached to the Women's Royal Almshouses, within the old Abbey walls. It has since disappeared
under unpleasantly mysterious circumstances.

(11) St. Cuthbert. About the early part of the 7th
century almost all Christian Churches in Britain had been
destroyed. Glastonbury, the origin of them all, remained.
So did the Church in Wales and Cornwall, and to some
extent in Strathclyde. And so also did some in Ireland,

[6] Cap. 12.

and in Scotland, Iona with its original settlements in Dalriada, and the Western Isles. Elsewhere the heathen were settling down quietly in possession. Gildas abuses the British, so full of missionary zeal, for not trying to convert their pagan conquerors (Bede, cap. 22). St. Gildas himself had been driven from the Isle of Steepholme, off the coast of the modern Weston-super-Mare, by Danish pirates. For a time he took refuge in Glastonbury Abbey. Till the time of St. Augustine's mission, there had been little clash between the Churches of Rome and Britain. His arrogance caused it. Imperial Rome fell in 510. Then the Bishop of Rome, constantly called by British abbots " the Abbot of Rome ", almost unconsciously assumed the Emperor's powers. It must be remembered that the Emperor Constantine commanded the first Church Council (since the one recorded in the Acts under St. James) at Arles in 314. and actually not only summoned the great Council of Nicaea in 325, but presided at it. And yet at Nicaea, out of 318 Bishops attending, not more than ten were Latin-speaking. At the Council of Byzantium or Constantinople in 337, Constantine having moved his imperial throne there, the Bishop of Constantinople actually presided, the Bishop of Rome being present. It really was the question of imperial centre. And Abbot Colman at the Synod of Whitby in 686 reminded it that the British Church had not sprung from St. Peter and Rome. The two Churches were sisters. During that century, in stirring times, St. Cuthbert was born, in 635. The pagan king Edwin of Northumbria had married Ethelberga (afterwards canonized, and the foundress of Ely), the daughter of King Ethelbert of Kent. Doubtless King Ethelbert's marriage to Queen Bertha, daughter of the Christian Gallican king, had something to do with the choice of Kent for St. Augustine's mission. St. Paulinus, St. Augustine's companion (afterwards Archbishop of York and Bishop of

Rochester), went north with Queen Ethelberga as her chaplain. Meantime Oswald, King Edwin's nephew, had taken refuge in Iona and been converted by the Celtic Church there. In 636, the year of St. Cuthbert's birth, Penda, King of Mercia, defeated and slew Edwin of Northumbria. In 635 Oswald, fresh from Iona, re-conquered Northumbria, and summoned missionaries from Iona to convert his subjects. The celebrated St. Aidan came. Oswald appointed him Bishop of Lindisfarne in 635. Bede tells us that while St. Aidan preached, King Oswald, who had learnt the language of the Scots at Iona, interpreted. St. Cuthbert was a pupil of St. Aidan. In 652, when seventeen, he decided to enter a monastery, and chose Melrose. When later Eata, the Abbot of Melrose, went to Ripon, he chose Cuthbert to be prior there. Oswald had been killed in battle, and his brother Oswy and Oswy's son Alfrid were kings in Northumbria. It was Alfrid who had asked St. Eata to go to Ripon. But Alfrid fell under the spell of that remarkable man, the pro-Roman Wilfrid, and the monastery was handed over to him. The great St. Hilda was cousin to Alfrid. She had educated St. Wilfrid in her monastery for monks and nuns. After the Council of Whitby in 664, which was swayed by Wilfrid, both St. Cuthbert and Abbot Colman with his Scottish monks returned to Lindisfarne, where St. Cuthbert became prior for twelve years, later being appointed bishop there by Oswy. In 676 St. Cuthbert went to live as a hermit on the island of Farne, to be alone with God and the sea. He remained there and thus till 684, when he became Bishop of Hexham, becoming next year Bishop of Lindisfarne. Meanwhile, in 668, the tactful and gifted Theodore of Tarsus came as Archbishop of Canterbury, whom Bede (Bk. 4, cap. 2) describes as "the first Archbishop whom all the English Church obeyed". He realized the value of Celtic monasteries as training schools, and of Celtic missionary zeal. Creating and confirming many bishoprics, he chose many Celtic-trained clergy like St. Cuthbert. King Oswy, lover of the Celtic Church, died in 670. Alfrid had been deposed by Oswy. Oswy's other son, Egfrith, succeeded. His mother Eanfleda, daughter of Edwin of Northumbria and St. Ethelberga, had inherited pro-Roman ways. In 684, Archbishop Theodore held a Synod at Twyford in Northumbria: King Egfrith presided. St. Cuthbert was unanimously chosen Bishop of Lindisfarne, and was with difficulty persuaded to consent. He showed his untrammelled originality and dedicated churches far out of his diocese, being dominated by his missionary spirit, to the annoyance of more rigid pro-Roman Bishops. Meantime Egfrith had made hostile expeditions to Ireland, and burnt their churches. In wrath, St. Cuthbert foresaw and foretold his death. In 685 the Picts, alarmed, rose in defence of their Church against St. Cuthbert's advice. Egfrith marched against them and was slain at Angus in Forfarshire. He was succeeded by an illegitimate half-brother, another Alfrid, who was foster-son of the great Adamnan, Abbot of Iona. Two years after St. Cuthbert was consecrated Bishop of Lindisfarne, weary, and probably foreseeing that death was near, he returned to his island of Farne in 687, and died there on March 20. His body was borne to Lindisfarne. Some 400 years later, in 1104, it was removed to Durham Cathedral. In 1826 his grave was opened. He was in his robes, and on his breast was a little stone travelling altar. In his day the age-long disputes between Celtic and Roman customs were healed. They had always clung to one Lord, one Faith. They had always been one Holy Catholic Church. Now, thanks to Theodore of Tarsus, and the consent of men like St. Cuthbert, minor differences were laid aside—alas to be re-awakened nearly 900 years later.

This is a short account of the Celtic Church in this land

and of a few of its countless saints, many of whose names still linger in place-names, a faint aroma of recollection. But in their day they made the desert blossom as a rose. The life of the seed sown is permanent. Verily they have their reward.